My Memoirs

How 'Change' brought Success into My 'Life'

Our Honeymoon Continues in Kashmir,
'Scary Days of my life' during Indo -Pak War,
and about many other challenges in my life.

Change is inevitable in Life
Change makes Life a success

GEORGE MALIAKAL

This Book edition is published in 2019 by
GLAN BOOKS
21 Uma Nagar, Thrissur 680655, Kerala, India.

Publishers and the Author acknowledge with thanks for the invaluable information that is available on the Internet. We also acknowledge with thanks and state hat some of the pictures included in this book are from the Internet and they are owned by the respective owners of their websites.

ISBN:
Price:

Dedicated
to
My Family

Mrs. Leela George

Contents

Capt. George Maliakal & Mrs. Leela George

Maj. George Maliakal & Mrs. Leela George

Preface

This book is very special to me. "My Memoirs – How Change brought Success in My Life" a unique book, which contains everything what you are looking for.

This will give the readers a new outlook about LIFE and CHANGE that can bring SUCCESS to you. Life, Change and Success are three keywords we all should worry about.

Change is inevitable in life. Change makes life a success. And this is applicable for everyone irrespective of our age, gender, cast o or religion or your nationality

This is true life story, how this young school teacher and a her college friend, undergoing officers training at Chennai, fall in love and they get married knowing well that her husband is an officer of the Indian army. It was their desire to live together after their marriage. So, she resigned her teaching job and wanted to be with her husband where he was posted and in which ever conditions he lived.

Since the officer was posted to a regiment near Srinagar, they plan to extend their honeymoon in Kashmir. Unfortunately, they get into big problems. Husband posted to a field unit could not take her with him. So, he had to find and solution to this. The situation along the international border with India and Pakistan worsens and they declared war against each other.

This young couple didn't know what to do? He was with his unit in the operational area and she was living all alone in Srinagar. Though she was advised to go back home in Kerala, she preferred to stay in Srinagar.
The content is about their extended honeymoon, the 'Scary days' she went through during the Indo-Pak War and many other challenging situations she lived through.

These events as such were written by me during some time after the 1971 Indo-Pak war, **about 45 years ago** and other details added to it later and edited now.

I can assure you this book will be exciting to read. This young lady is my wife.

George Maliakal
Author

Life Journey Begins

The Beginning

The guard blew a long whistle, waved his green flag signalling the engine driver his clearance to start the train. The train, giving out a long siren, started moving off the platform. Standing at the door of the first- class compartment, we bid farewell to our parents, brothers, sisters and friends, who had come to the station to see us off. It was a sad moment; as the train started moving, we saw their worry and concern, unable to control their feelings in parting us, a scene which we just couldn't forget. Even, we felt our loneliness as the train picked up speed.

However, the hope of beginning an eventful family life together gave us a reason for joy. We were leaving our home, for the time being, only to have come back later - may be after a couple of years. We were beginning to live our life together. from both our families in the Defence, thus, they did not know 'anything' whatsoever, about the systems, set up and social life specially in the army.

My in laws were very confident that their son, George, my husband would be able to take care of me and face any challenges of his profession. Whereas, my parents and my relatives were really worried over the fact, that their daughter was leaving them to go to the northernmost part of India and stay there in a separated family quarter, all alone. At the same time, the fact that their daughter was accompanying her smart, young, able husband, who was a Captain in the Indian Army, gave them confidence about the future and safety of their daughter.

It was a move from the southernmost part to the northernmost part of our country, thousands of miles away, away from our home and relatives, to set up 'a home away from home'. Well, that is life.

We went to our coupe, checked our luggage once again, ensured everything was OK; and settled down. Oh! what a relief! We both were so tired in getting our things ready. It certainly called for a break. Preparations were on for days to get set for such a living.

There wasn't anyone there at Srinagar known to us from our State to look forward to in case any need arises. Therefore, we had to plan everything in such a way that we were able to manage things ourselves. We had also decided to take a pet, a puppy just born and not even opened her eyes, as our best companion, specially so to me, during her stay alone at Srinagar.

I vividly remember the evening on the day before our departure it was really a small gathering of both our families, at my in laws house, showing everything that we were planning to carry with us and my husband was explaining how we plan to manage things there, to our parents and relatives and giving them confidence that everything was going to be all right. We had a lot of luggage to carry, that too, over thousands of miles, including a number of transhipments en route.

"How is our little one?" I asked my husband. He checked inside the small card board box in which we had placed our little pup, wrapped in some fine towel to keep herself warm. She was sleeping in the warmth of the towel, as if she was sleeping with her mother; not aware of the fact that she was being taken over thousands of miles away to the northernmost state of India, Jammu and Kashmir. She was blind and would have taken a few more days before she opened her eyes; a black cute little thing. We had not taken any tickets for her and so we had to carry her more safely, undetected by the railway staff.

The train was going at a comfortable speed; being in a coupe we had full privacy except when the train ticket examiner or the waiter from the train dining car disturbed us. It was an evening train from our place. In those days, the distance from Thrissur to Pathankot, the northernmost railway terminal, was covered in three segments. From Thrissur to Madras, from Madras to Delhi and from Delhi to Pathankot. Instead of a through train, there was only a direct coach from here to Delhi via Madras.

Though our train would reach Madras in the morning, the direct coach would be attached either to the Grand Trunk express or to the Dakshin Express going to Delhi in the afternoon. It took two nights and two days to reach Delhi. So, in all it would take three nights and almost three days to reach Delhi. Further, from Delhi to Pattankot it was an overnight journey. It looked as if we had a long holiday to be spent in train. Now a days, there are through trains to link far distant places. Even, there is a train from the southernmost state of Kerala to Jammu Tawi, the farthest railway terminal in the northernmost state, Jammu and Kashmir.

Someone knocked at our door; husband opened the door; it was the ticket examiner. He came inside with his chart, checked our ticket and looked at our luggage. Seeing the volume of our luggage he asked my husband whether we had weighed our luggage and paid for any extra luggage. When my husband showed him the receipt, he was quite satisfied. He closed the door behind him and came back and sat at his place.

By now the train had passed a few local stations; it was going at a higher speed only to halt at the next main station. Golden rays of the setting sun against the moving train, entered our coupe through the windows and brightened our cabin. Out in the open, we saw green paddy fields with their leaves moving along with the direction of the wind, a graceful movement. A waiter from the train catering service knocked at our door and asked, "Dinner Sir?" Coming from home we had carried our dinner and so we told him, "No, thanks".

We could sense some movements inside the card board box; we looked in; the little one was moving around searching for a feed from her mother, poor fellow. I took her out, kept the puppy on my lap and gave her a feed from the baby feeding bottle we had carried with us. Without any fuss she sucked from the bottle; we replaced the cloth inside the box and put her back to sleep.

Then he told me, "You better take care of the little one, OK? She is the one going to be your best companion during your stay at Srinagar." I looked at him smiled and said "I know, I shall take care of her; I really love her." Thus, our love for pets began. Since we were quite tired, we had early dinner and went to bed early. It was quite an enjoyable night.

We were woken up by some vendor shouting out side "Chai, chai, chai - coffee." my husband opened the window shutter which we had pulled down for security reasons; it was some station in Tamil Nadu; we were nearing Madras, now Chennai; maybe it was another one-hour distance or so. He pulled down the shutter and went back to bed. Actually, I was half a sleep. The train reached Madras Central Station, now reamed as Chennai Central Station.

It was a major railway junction in South India; it was also one of the nerve centres of railway movements. Within seconds our train became empty; all passengers got down except those travelling in the 'through compartments'. Those who got down from the train were moving in such a hurry to reach their destinations; and some waited there at the platform for their friends and relatives. A few minutes later, a railway engine came and pulled our compartment to another track, to be attached to the Delhi bound train later in the afternoon.

We had enough time to freshen ourselves. With our luggage and the little one, we didn't want to go anywhere. So, we spent our time in our coupe and on the platform. It was a long wait. Later in the afternoon, our 'through compartment' was taken out and attached to the Delhi bound Grand Trunk Express train.

This was a much faster train and was to reach its destination Delhi on the morning of the day after; another two nights and two days stay in the train. Along this route, the train would stop only on very important stations. This train was going to cover a major part of our journey, across our country and we were much exited.

The train left Madras around tea time. The Train Ticket Examiner came and checked our tickets once again; this time too we were very careful about our pup. Once again, we were alone in the coupe, we had plenty of time with us to relax and to ride through our sweet memories.

We just couldn't believe that we were married and that I was accompanying my husband to his place of work. In him I found a Man of my choice with the qualities that I have been looking for, and similarly, he found in me his Dream girl with everything he has been looking for. We had liked each other, we loved each other and we always wished to get married; it was a long wait, which culminated into our marriage. Oh! It was so beautiful memory of events.

Second part of our journey -
Chennai to New Delhi

Our First Meeting.
It all began quite unexpected. During the final year of my Bachelor degree I decided to go for an additional coaching in my main subject, Mathematics. It was a coaching class for both girls and boys; and was just for a period of three months only, something like a refreshing class just before the exams. There were lots of girls and boys in the class and I had a few selected friends, boys and girls; and my husband was one among them. We used to discuss mathematical problems, and even exchange our notes. It was just a simple friendship and there was nothing beyond that. And surprisingly after our tuition classes were over, I had never met him.

It was my dream to become High School Teacher. So, after I finished my degree, I applied for a teaching job. Since my subject was Maths, it was comparatively easy to get a teaching post of a Maths teacher. And I was very lucky. I got a teaching job as a High School Maths teacher in one of the Convent Girls' High

School, near Thrissur.

One day, sometime during December 1966, I received a greeting card by post. When I looked at the from address, I found that it was from Mr George, my friend at the tuition class. It looked quite normal. On the card he had wished me Xmas greetings and also found a letter addressed to me. It was something like a surprise gift from one of my dear friends. I read it very fast, in the letter he had written about all that happened after we left the tuition class.

I knew, during his college days he was very active and very popular. He was the Senior Under Officer of their College NCC. He had also represented Kerala State, NCC at the Republic Day parade at Delhi in 1965. He was also their college Hockey Team Captain, and he was also very good at the extempore speech competitions, etc.

From his letter, I could make out that, it was his dream to join the armed forces as commissioned officer. It looked as if his destiny was with him. He got selected as SSC (NT-3) and presently he was undergoing Training at the Officer's Training School (OTS) at Madras, later renamed as Chennai, from September 1966 and will become a Commissioned Officer of the Indian Army in August 1967.

He had also written little about his routine there Training at the Officers' Training School was really very tough, a busy schedule with very little time to yourself. Life there was something like a machine, following a set routine with very few changes. He said he never got time so he could write to his parents only. So it was to compensate for the loss he decided to send at least X' Mas greetings to his friends with a small note in it.

The list included among others, two of his good girl friends with whom he was more friendly during his Maths coaching class. One of them was this was me, who later became his life partner. In return what he had expected from them was just a reply acknowledging my greetings; at the same time, he was not sure to get a reply from these girls.

I was quite happy that he had not forgotten me. I liked the content of his letter and. Replied to his letter congratulating him for getting his dream profession giving details of my activities here.

Getting Closer to Each Other.
May be after a couple of weeks or so I received a second letter from him. In my reply I mentioned that I was quite surprised that he could find some time to write to me I also wished him good luck. It was a mere exchange of information, beginning of a healthy friendship.

I received a couple of more letters from him. In his every letter I found something that had attracted me. As we continued to correspond each other I started liking him, something more than a normal friendship. I found his letters giving me an encouragement in life; appreciated his efforts for a better future. I was really surprised to receive letters regularly and I also replied to him.

I found his letters made me feel quite comfortable. I strongly started feeling that there was something in him that attracted me towards him; from his letters I could understand, even he felt the same. We were getting closer to each other.

I realised that I started loving him; and from his letters I sensed the same, he too loved me. I saw everything that I looked for in him. I got a feeling that he could be the best choice as my life partner. We were of the same age; we both belonged to middle class Christian families and happened to be from the same town. Without any hesitation I expressed my desire to marry him, in a way it was my own decision.

It was as if he had been waiting for such a proposal from my side; he wholeheartedly accepted my proposal. He was mighty happy; again, it was his own decision. Thus, we had now mutually decided to get married. It was an understanding between two of us. Now I was already teaching and he was yet to become a Commissioned Officer. We decided to wait; our regular correspondence continued.

On the sixth of August of 1967, he was commissioned as an officer in the Corps of Engineers. The 'Pipping Ceremony' was at midnight after a late dinner party

2/Lt. G. C. Maliakal

at the Officer's Mess. More than five hundred cadets were commissioned in to the Army as officers. I was so happy to hear that news. In fact, I felt very proud of him. He was granted a few days joining time and a short leave before we joined our respective units.

I knew he would be coming home for a few days; so, we decided to meet each other when he arrives for a few days. But due to some unforeseen events. I could not come home; thus, we could not meet each other. He returned to his unit where he was posted after he was commissioned as an commissioned officer. Later he joined the No. 41YO's (Young Officer's Course) Course, at the College of Military Engineering (CME) at Pune. We didn't lose our heart; we took it as our fate. But we wrote to each other very regularly. After his YO's course was over, he was posted to a Regiment, which was located in Kashmir valley, an operational area.

After teaching at convent school teaching in the convent Girl's High School for one year, I joined for a degree in Bachelor of Education (B.Ed.); one-year course, which would make me a qualified teacher at the high school grade.

In 1968 end, when he came on my annual leave, we made it a point to meet each other. It was our first meeting, a meeting after waiting so long, and when we met, you know what could have happened. As the saying goes, 'When heart is full, words are few', we just couldn't express ourselves. During his leave we met on a few more occasions. These meetings were confidential and no one else knew about them. And he went back after his leave.

In one of my letters to him, I expressed my desire to get married at the earliest, as my parents were now planning for my marriage. At the same time, it was his desire to get married after he became a Captain in the army. I appreciated his decision and wrote to him that I would manage the things at my home. I was prepared to wait. Our regular correspondence kept us closer and closer. We knew each other very well.

In June 1969, he was promoted to the rank of Captain in the army. And when had come on his annual leave in1969; we decided to inform our parents of our desire and decision to get married. And we sought their approval and blessing. We were quite anxious to know their reaction. As generally parents do, they asked us to do a rethinking and then take a decision. We must appreciate their love and affection and concern for their children. They gave their full consent for our marriage. Our happiness found no bounds; we were going to get married. It was only a question of certain formalities.

Our families interacted and had made all arrangements for our marriage. We thanked God. He came home, after a short course of three months at Faizabad, near Lucknow, on April 22nd 1970, a Wednesday, the day of our engagement ceremony. As per the Christian custom then, in an arranged marriage, the boy met the girl at the girl's place and expressed their willingness; and later they had their engagement ceremony at the church.

After the engagement, there was a public announcement, in the parish church of both the boy and the girl, about the proposed marriage alliance on three consecutive Sundays, after the holy mass. The purpose of this announcement was to let the public know of the proposed marriage alliance, so that if anyone had any objection, they could lodge their complaints and the church would take appropriate action as deemed fit.

In our case, since he had come on forty five days leave, we got exempted from this lengthy procedure and all the three public announcements were made on the same Sunday, April 26th, and our marriage was fixed for April 27th, Monday; so that we could get more days together after our marriage before he returned to his Regiment.

Wedding Bells Ring.
Our wedding was at 9.30 a.m. on April 27th 1970 at the Lourdes Cathedral at Thrissur. The actual wedding ceremony takes place in the middle of the holy mass. In the beginning, the 'Thali', what we call 'Mangal Sutra' in the Hindu culture, wedding rings and the 'best dress' he offered to me, were blessed by the priest. Then we were told to hold our right hand together and the priest blessed us. Later was the sacred function.

I was asked to kneel down; and the 'best woman' lifted my wedding net from behind giving a free space for him tie the wedding knot with the 'Thali' around my neck. He tied the wedding knot; and placed the best dress, a saree on her head, which was later taken and put around my left hand. He then put the blessed wedding ring with his name on my finger and I put the blessed wedding ring with my name on his finger. The holy mass continued. At the end, there was a final blessing. We then signed in the marriage register of the church. It was the end of the wedding ceremony inside the church.

When we came out of the church, everyone congratulated us and wished a happy married life.

Lourdes Cathedral Church at Thrissur

This followed reception at our houses. And as per the custom, I stayed at my husband's house. Finally, we were married, our dream came true. We both relished our sweet memories. It gave us a feeling as if we were just married. He held me close and kissed me; it was a moment of celebration of the fulfilment of our desire.

Captain George Maliakal & Mrs. Leela George

Learning about Army Life

The train was moving faster. We gave another feed to our little fellow; she had still not opened her eyes. We decided to take some rest before we had our dinner. It was dinner time when the train stopped at the next major station. We had ordered our dinner and it was served in our coupe. It was our second night together in the train; another enjoyable night. It was a late morning for us; the waiter served us bed coffee; we freshened ourselves and had our breakfast. At the next station he bought a newspaper and a couple of magazines.

I knew he was posted to an Engineer Regiment near Pattan, a place about 40 Km west of Srinagar. Since his regiment was located in the 'Operational rea', families were not allowed there. However, he was allowed to keep his family in separated family quarters at Srinagar and therefore, he had requested for a separated family quarter for me.

Since there was no vacant accommodation then available for allotment, he was allowed to bring his family, me and make my own arrangements for accommodation. 'Separated Family Quarters' / means, quarters generally built at selected stations, where the defence personnel could keep their families while they served in the 'Field'/operational areas. Thus, he had to make his own arrangements and had hired a flat in a building in Rajbagh area, a nice residential area of Srinagar.

Srinagar being close to his unit in field area, as a special case, officers who had their families at Srinagar were allowed to visit their families on weekends. He could leave his unit on Saturday afternoon and report back on duty on Monday morning. That means, I had to stay at Srinagar away from my husband during the whole week, anxiously waiting for him to come on the weekends

I was a double graduate, B.Sc., B.Ed., was already teaching at a convent girls' high school at the time of our marriage. After our marriage, we always wanted to be together, sharing our love and concern for each other, taking care of my husband our house and later our children. Therefore, we jointly decided that I should resign my job and join him wherever he was posted.
We knew, we were taking a great risk; because had I continued my job, we could have some substantial savings for our future. But what we preferred was, a real happy family life than some monetary gains. Thus, I was all set to join him even under the above circumstances.
 How do I spend the whole week and that too alone in a flat? So, we had to find something to keep me busy through the week. Finally, he succeeded in finding a teaching job for me at the famous Presentation Convent Girls' High school at Rajbagh in Srinagar, a prestigious institution, only at a walking distance from our hired house.
The house had three stories, the ground floor was already rented out to another army officer's family, we had hired the middle floor and the landlord had occupied the top floor. Further, the landlord had one of his sons was also serving in the army and had two

26

daughters. Thus, it was after arranging a job and a house that he had come home on his annual leave. And I was so thrilled to accompany him after the leave and when he told me that a teaching job was already waiting for her, I jumped with joy and had hugged him.

I was keen to know something more about the army life. So, I asked him, 'Please, tell me something about the life in the army and the family life.', Till now, it was through his letters only I had some idea about the army. Now that I was going to live with me, I had already become part of the whole organisation and therefore, I wanted to know everything possible that a wife of an army officer should know, so that I could be a successful wife of a successful army officer and we had plenty of time at our disposal to discuss.

He gave me a brief account of everything about army, its life style, both in a peace station as well as in a field station; the family life, officers mess functions and so on - things which I was never accustomed to.

When he had finished explaining, he found me worrying over something and he knew it was the sense of fear, whether I would be able to live up to his expectation, that was worrying her; but, he was quite confident that I would prove to be a wonderful housewife in the new set up. Smiling at me he told, "Don't you worry, you can make it and you will make it." I smiled at him and said, "I hope so."

By now, the train had passed through a number of states across the country. We could see the difference in their culture, in their dress, in the edible items available on the platform, in their language and so on. It was a wonderful experience specially to me.

It was more than two and half days after we left our home and there was still a long way to go. We spent another night in the train, next day morning the train wouldtake us to New Delhi.

Our train reached Agra on next day morning. It was only a few hours run from there to Delhi. Agra was a historical place in India, where stood one of the wonders of the world, the famous Taj Mahal, a great monument built by the emperor Shajahan in memory of his late queen Noorjahan. It was a major station; it also had a number of defence units located there. We saw a lot of tourists there on the platform who had come to the old city to visit Taj Mahal and other historical places.

A glance at Thaj Mahal

Taj mahal

We visited a few places in and around New Delhi

February 1971, it was quite cold in Delhi. We spent a couple of days in Delhi at the retiring room of the New Delhi railway station and visited almost all places of tourist attraction. While we were in Delhi, our pup had opened her eyes and started seeing the outside world. We called her Patty.

Now that she could see, she started moving around and we had to give her more care. When we went for visiting places, we left her in our room. We visited only those places which were in and around Delhi; because of our tight schedule. So, we decided to visit places like Kuthab Minar, Fathepur city and Taj Mahal, on some other occasion.

We started the third leg of our train journey from New Delhi to Pathankot, the last railway terminal in the northern direction in those days; it was an overnight journey. The train usually left in the evening. It passed through the states of Haryana and Punjab and some important stations before it reached Pathankot railway station in the morning.

The scene at Pathankot railway station was quite different from other stations we had seen en-route. The passengers comprised of civilians and mostly defence personnel; Officers, JCO's and men in their uniform and some of them with their families, like me. It looked almost like a military station. Pathankot was the nearest railway station for all those troops deployed in Jammu and Kashmir sector; and therefore, there was quite a heavy movement of troops through this station. We reported to the Officers Transit Camp, near to the railway station, who then arranged for our onward journey to Srinagar.

Our Journey from Pathankot to Srinagar was by road and it was covered in two days; on the first day from Pathankot to Udhampur and on the second day from Udhampur to Srinagar. For this purpose, the army had their own buses, old modified types as well as new ones. Our luggage was carried in trucks. Even officers who had to travel beyond Srinagar to Sonamarg, Kargil and Leh, followed the same route except that they had to travel additional days depending upon their destination

We were about twenty-five to thirty, including families, to go to Udhampur. Hence a regular new bus was detailed for our journey from Pathankot to Udhampur. We took our pup along with us inside the bus; we didn't forget to fill the feeding bottle with milk and had carried some towels; something that parents ensured while taking their children along with them. Some of other families inside the bus knew that we were carrying a pup with us; and when they were told that we were bringing it from such a far of place Kerala, they were really surprised.

The journey from Pathankot commenced by about 9.30 a.m. or so, along the Pathankot - Jammu national highway. We had our lunch en route at the transit officers' mess at Samba. We, the officers did not have to pay for our food as we were authorised free ration in the field areas; whereas we had to pay for our families. We reached Udhampur via Jammu, in the evening and the journey was quite OK. At the Officers mess at Udhampur, we were allotted a room; and we stayed the night there. We had our evening tea, dinner and next day morning breakfast from the mess. It was our fifth night after we left our home; yet we were far away from our final destination. So far so good, even the little one seemed to be enjoying the trip.

Next day, we started our onward journey from Udhampur to Srinagar at about 7 a.m. after breakfast; this time it was in a modified officer's bus. We did not forget to carry the essentials for our little companion, pup; this time, we had taken some additional clothing because we knew it would be too cold for me. He was were wearing his winter uniform whereas I was wearing our traditional dress saree, and a woollen sweater. We had also kept a woollen shawl and a pair of woollen gloves for me. Being winter time, it would much colder.

We followed the national highway. It was a well-designed mountain highway meeting the demands of the heavy traffic along that route; all along, it either climbed up or down the big mountains. I was getting exposed to a lot of new experiences in my life. It was the only land route from Jammu to Srinagar, the life line to Kashmir. Along the route, we saw landslides at a few places which always became the bottle necks, restricting the up and down traffic.

The road passed through some important places like Kud, Pattni Top, Ramban, Battode, Banihal Pass (Jawahar Tunnel), Quasikund, Ananthanag, and onward to Srinagar. It was not a comfortable ride as compared to the previous day. Being a mountain road, the bus swung to right and left as it negotiated the curves and this forced us to have a firm grip against being thrown out of our seats; a real strain to your hands.

Our lunch halt was at the Transit Officers' mess at

Ramban; after a quick freshening break, we started off. During this short break, somehow, we had managed to take care of our pup and had finished feeding her.

It still had not snowed in the Kashmir valley; but the weather was so cold and chill that it had all the symptoms of a snow fall any day. Sometime after we left Ramban, we found some changes in the weather.

The sunny weather had faded away now; sky was overcast. It looked as if it was going to rain. We felt very cool breeze through the windows of our bus; we closed all of them. As we moved on, we still felt chill wind blowing across entering through the small openings of the old bus. It was becoming very cold. I wore the shawl over her woollen sweater. I also wore my woollen gloves.

We were nearing Banihal Pass where the great Jawahar tunnel linked the two regions, Jammu and Kashmir. It had also started raining and we cannot just forget the plight of the officers and their families, holding their umbrellas opened inside the officer's bus to save themselves from getting wet; because it was an old modified bus and was leaking very badly.

Everyone wanted to reach Srinagar early. But the day long journey passing through places like Kud, Ramban, Battode, Banihal pass, Quasikund, Ananthanag, and onward to Srinagar could not have taken less.

Travelling through Jawhar Tunnel, one of the longest tunnels in the country, at an altitude of over 10,000 ft., was an experience by itself. When we crossed the tunnel, we had entered the Kashmir valley. After descending the mountain, we reached a place called

Entry to the Tunnel from Jam mu side. Exit of the Tunnel to Kashmir side and a view of the inside

Quasikund, where we all had hot cup of tea. It made us little warm from inside, but outside, it was very cold. Finally, we reached the officers' transit camp at Srinagar about 5 p.m. in the evening.

Finally reached our destination.
It was still raining and was very chill, an indication of a snowfall. Our unit vehicle had come to take us to our house at Rajbagh. inally, we had reached our destination, away from our home, *after spending five days and five nights of travelling*, excluding the two days we spent at Delhi for sight- seeing. There, we were given a rousing warm welcome by the landlord and his family; they insisted us to join them for dinner. We enjoyed their hospitality.

It was exceptionally cold in the night, difficult to manage specially for me, who had come from a tropical area to a place where it was almost going to snow. Anyway, having foreseen this eventuality, he had the 'American sleeping bag', feather filled and light weight, which he used in the high-altitude area. Thus, we really enjoyed the warmth; and didn't know what was happening outside.
It was a very late morning and when we opened the curtains of our windows, we were really thrilled to see the outside world - it was all looking white, the ground, the trees, the roofs, everything; because it had snowed during the night and it was still snowing. A feeling we got that even the nature was so happy and welcomed us into the Kashmir valley for an enjoyable stay. And thus, our family life began, just two of us, 'A home away from home'.

When we opened our widow, we saw our neighbourhood was completely covered with snow. For me, this was first experience in my life, to see, feel and enjoy in snow.

Ourr First Winter in Kashmir (1971)

This was our first winter together; and so, everything that was happening during this winter was, all new to me. We came out of our house to feel the cold outside and to feel the snow. I touched the snow, picked up some in my bare hand. I was so thrilled; immediately I felt the freezing temperature in my hand. When it had stopped snowing, we spent some more time playing in snow, first time experience in my life.

In winter, prior to a snow fall, the weather becomes very cold and with rain it becomes chill before it starts snowing. It was very nice to watch the snow falling. Snow in flake form comes from heaven and falls on the ground. Initially, flakes falling on the ground immediately melts away till the ground temperature becomes zero degree Celsius. Then on, these flakes stay on the ground as it is. And after sometime, as the snow fall continues the ground gets covered with snow, like a white carpet. The sight of snow fall is like somebody letting the fine cotton out

Outside view when we opened our window

Our First Winter in Kashmir (1971)

This was our first winter together; and so, everything that was happening during this winter was, all new to me. We came out of our house to feel the cold outside and to feel the snow. I touched the snow, picked up some in my bare hand. I was so thrilled; immediately I felt the freezing temperature in my hand. When it had stopped snowing, we spent some more time playing in snow, first time experience in my life.

In winter, prior to a snow fall, the weather becomes very cold and with rain it becomes chill before it starts snowing. It was very nice to watch the snow falling. Snow in flake form comes from heaven and falls on the ground. Initially, flakes falling on the ground immediately melts away till the ground temperature becomes zero degree Celsius. Then on, these flakes stay on the ground as it is. And after sometime, as the snow fall continues the ground gets covered with snow, like a white carpet. The sight of snow fall is like somebody letting the fine cotton out of a big pillow from a height.

During heavy snow fall, the visibility becomes very poor and the vehicles use yellow fog lights. You don't get wet while walking on the road when it is snowing; so, you don't need an umbrella, but of course you need a hat. However, after sometime, fresh snow would start setting on your dress and you need to remove it. He still had a few more days left before he joined duty. So, before he joined his regiment, we tried to arrange our house. Weather was very chill.

House Warming.

It is not the same kind of 'house warming' I am referring to. I am talking of the heating arrangements inside the house during winter. In Western countries, this is done by using oil firing burners generally kept in the basements with hot air circulation arrangements inside the house, or by other central heating arrangements. Whereas in Kashmir, people used 'Bukhari' an arrangement to burn wood / steam coal /or kerosene.

It is a drum like thing with legs, openings and exhaust gas pipes with air regulator. And we needed one such thing for one room. We had 'bukharies' with steam coal burning arrangements. Once you know how to operate, it becomes simple. And if you do not know, you had it, the smoke which is full of carbon monoxide can fill your room and choke you to death. Such incidents had happened in the past. He taught me how to light our 'bukhari', so that I could light it confidently in my absence. He was glad; or else he would have been worrying about my safety and fire hazard.

Before he joined duty, we went to the Presentation Convent where he had arranged a job for me. Met their Mother Superior and Head Mistress. They were happy to meet me. They asked me to join duty on the school reopening day sometime during first week of April. Generally, the schools reopened between end of March to beginning of April, depending on the snow fall. The school was at a walking distance from our house. Everything was set. He had to return to his unit to join duty.

Separation was quite unbearable to both of us. Though this was known to happen, we still felt very sad. He consoled me that it was a matter of a few days after he would be back home again during the next weekend and that there was nothing to worry. Even our landlord came down and gave me a fatherly advice and assurance of my safety. Finally, he left for his unit.

In Srinagar, sometime we used to have one foot or even more, of standing snow on the ground. It was real fun playing in the snow; of course, we have to put on enough warm clothing to feel comfortable. For getting a better effect, clothes are worn in various layers to maintain more warmth. This is the time I learnt knitting from landlord's daughters.

We used to play in the snow lying in our courtyard, running, throwing snow balls at each other. We also made several models and once we made a model of a Sphinx and sat between its hands. Oh! it was real fun. We still remember our good old days.

This was my first life experience to watch snow falls, touch and feel the snow and also to play in snow. It was a wonderful feeling I had.

Initially, for a moment I doubted my decision whether it was right or wrong to resign my teaching job in Kerala and to accompany my husband wherever he was posted and live together thorough out our life.

Until he told me that he had already arranged for a teaching job at a Convent school nearby, when he came for our engagement ceremony, I was feeling little worried thinking what would I do when my goes back to his unit and till he returned on Saturday afternoon on weekend. But after he I told me that he after evaluating the situation that when he returned to his unit how would I be spending during the whole week till he came back on next weekend.

He knew it would be very difficult for me, especially so, since I was new to that place, and didn't have any friends to talk to. So, what he had told me then was, he found a two-way solution to this unique problem. No1. Solution was, to find a teaching job somewhere there nearby. This would keep me busy from Monday to Friday during the school hours and my other commitments to my students and for my school activities would also keep me busy for some more time. Then, I also need to spend time for my personal things like, preparing food for myself, and taking care of the house will also keep me busy for a few more hours in a day/night, But what would I do during the balance hours? Also, on school holidays etc?

And the second way to solve this issue, Even if I get a teaching job, how would I live alone there, whether it is a house or a flat? He had quick solution for this, - to take a puppy with us. So, now I have to take care of the puppy, and in turn the puppy will keep me busy and company. The puppy you busy. Further, I could follow the tips how to manage the puppy and he was quite sure that I would be able to manage everything well.

After finishing his long planning, he looked at me and had asked, "What do you think about my plan?"
His planning looked to me quite alright. I told him, "I think it's workable solution and is ok for me." Suddenly another thought came to my mind. I told

him, "But you I cannot handle big dogs. It must be a small variety." I expressed my concern.

"Yes, I quite agree with you." he told me. A small breed so that you will be able to manage it." We must take a eI agree with you got your point."   can understand your point I Can understand.?

He held my hands and told me, 'I am glad you appreciated my effort, lack sleepless nights thinking, 'how do I find the solution. And finally, I found a way out. I am glad."

Luckily, we got a good pup from one of her uncles. It was a bitch, fully black and had, not even opened her eyes, a black cute little thing Later we named her a Patty, and she was the first member of our pet dog family. Thus, we decided to take her when he returned to his regiment after finishing his annual.

Both of us knew that it was our mutual interest that after our wedding we wanted to live together wherever he was posted, whatever conditions.be. It was our mutual responsibility to understand each other and support each other and make our life beautiful live a happy making our life more beautiful.

Patty was growing up in the new environment; she was not aware of the fact that she was migrated from a tropical area to a snowbound area; however, she got used to it. he gradually taught her the basic lessons. We were staying in the middle floor for which we had a *sit out*. Still we had to train Patty to go down after its meal for her natures' calls; we found her very smart and intelligent. I used to tie her in the *sit out* during the day and inside the bed room at night.

We named her Patty. Patty started recognising the inmates of that building and started barking at the strangers /visitors. I gave Patty full attention and care; I knew Patty had already started proving her worth as my best companion and body guard.

Silver Salver.

Whenever an officer of our Regiment got married, it was customary to give a warm reception to the newly married couple at our officer's mess, at the earliest opportunity after their marriage and give them a special wedding gift. And if by chance the wife was unable to join the officer at the regimental location, the gift was then presented to the officer at a function organised at the officer's mess.

The wedding gift of his Regiment was a specially designed one - a beautiful six inches diameter silver salver, with the matter engraved in it, as 'Presented to (name of the Officer), by the Officers and their Families of (name of unit) Regiment, on (date, month and year). Further, it became more special with the signatures, of all officers held on the strength of the regiment on that date, engraved inside all around the main matter. Thus, the wedding gift had an immense value as it was an expression of their love and affection towards you and it made you remember your good old days in the regiment.

In our case, this invaluable wedding gift was presented to me d
during a mess function organised at his Officer's mess at Pattan soon after we had reached Srinagar

after our marriage, in early 1971.

There were twenty-one signatures engraved in our silver salver. And it was a token of their love and affection. We still recognise those signatures and their names even after a long spell of Forty-Nine years of our married life.

It was one of the wonderful gifts we have ever received in our life - a wonderful gesture from our brother officers and their families; because in a regiment, we always considered it as a family and it was always 'A Home Away from Our Sweet Home' for each of us.

Our Wedding Gift - Silver Salver

Our Puppy Patty - **Sharing moments with her**

Playing in Snow

Presentation Convent High School
where I was teaching

Spending Quality Time with Patty

need a hat. However, after sometime, fresh snow would start setting on your dress and you need to remove it. He still had a few more days left before he joined duty. So, before he joined his regiment, we tried to arrange our house. Weather was very chill.

It is a drum like thing with legs, openings and exhaust gas pipes with air regulator. And we needed one such thing for one room. We had *'bukharies'* with steam coal burning arrangements. Once you know how to operate, it becomes simple. And if you do not know, you had it, the smoke which is full of carbon monoxide can fill your room and choke you to death. Such It is a drum like thing with legs, openings and exhaust gas pipes with air regulator. And we needed one such thing for one room.

We had *'bukharies'* with steam coal burning arrangements. Once you know how to operate, it becomes simple. And if you do not know, you had it, the smoke which is full of carbon monoxide can fill your room and choke you to death. Such incidents had happened in the past. He taught me how to light our *'bukhari'*, so that I could light it confidently in my absence. He was glad; or else he would have been worrying about my safety and fire hazard.

Before he joined duty, we went to the Presentation Convent where he had arranged a job for me. Met their Mother Superior and Head Mistress. They were happy to meet me. They asked me to join duty on the school reopening day sometime during first week of April. Generally, the schools reopened between end of March to beginning of April, depending

Separation was quite unbearable to both of us. Though this was known to happen, we still felt very sad. He consoled me that it was a matter of a few days after he would be back home again during the next weekend and that there was nothing to worry. Even our landlord came down and gave me a fatherly advice and assurance of my safety. Finally, he left for his unit.

In Srinagar, sometime we used to have one foot or even more, of standing snow on the ground. It was real fun playing in the snow; of course, we have to put on enough warm clothing to feel comfortable. For getting a better effect, clothes are worn in various layers to maintain more warmth. This is the time I learnt knitting from landlord's daughters.

We used to play in the snow lying in our courtyard, running, throwing snow balls at each other. We also made several models and once we made a model of a Sphinx and sat between its hands. Oh! it was real fun. We still remember our good old days.

This was my first life experience to watch snow falls, touch and feel the snow and also to play in snow. It was a wonderful feeling I had.

Initially, for a moment I doubted my decision whether it was right or wrong to resign my teaching job in Kerala and to accompany my husband wherever he was posted and live together thorough out our life.

Until he told me that he had already arranged for a

teaching job at a Convent school nearby, when he came for our engagement ceremony, I was feeling little worried thinking what would I do when my goes back to his unit and till he returned on Saturday afternoon on weekend. But after he I told me that he after evaluating the situation that when he returned to his unit how would I be spending during the whole week till he came back on next weekend.

He knew it would be very difficult for me, especially so, since I was new to that place, and didn't have any friends to talk to. So, what he had told me then was, he found a two-way solution to this unique problem.

No1. Solution was, to find a teaching job somewhere there nearby. This would keep me busy from Monday to Friday during the school hours and my other commitments to my students and for my school activities would also keep me busy for some more time. Then, I also need to spend time for my personal things like, preparing food for myself, and taking care of the house will also keep me busy for a few more hours in a day/night, But what would I do during the balance hours? Also, on school holidays etc?

And the second way to solve this issue, Even if I get a teaching job, how would I live alone there, whether it is a house or a flat? He had quick solution for this, - to take a puppy with us. So, now I have to take care of the puppy, and in turn the puppy will keep me busy and company. Further, I could follow the tips how to manage the puppy and he was quite sure that I would be able to manage everything well.

After finishing his long planning, he looked at me and had asked, "What do you think about my plan?"

His planning looked to me quite alright. I told him, "I think it's workable solution and is ok for me." Suddenly another thought came to my mind. I told him, "But you I cannot handle big dogs. It must be a small variety." I expressed my concern.

"Yes, I quite agree with you." he told me. A small breed so that you will be able to manage it." We must take a eI agree with you got your point." can understand your point I Can understand.?

He held my hands and told me, 'I am glad you appreciated my effort. I have had sleepless nights thinking, 'how do I find the solution. And finally, I found a way out. I am glad."

Luckily, we got a good pup from one of her uncles. It was a bitch, fully black and had, not even opened her eyes, a black cute little thing Later we named her a Patty, and she was the first member of our pet dog family. Thus, we decided to take her when he returned to his regiment after finishing his annual.

Both of us knew that it was our mutual interest that after our wedding we wanted to live together wherever he was posted, whatever conditions.be. It was our mutual responsibility to understand each other and support each other and make our life beautiful live a happy making our life more beautiful.

Patty was growing up in the new environment; she was not aware of the fact that she was migrated from a tropical area to a snowbound area; however, she got used to it. he gradually taught her the basic lessons. We were staying in the middle floor for which we had a *sit out*. Still we had to train Patty to go down after its meal for her natures' calls; we found her very smart

Capt. George Maliakal & Mrs. Leela George

and intelligent. I used to tie her in the *sit out* during the day and inside the bed room at night.

We named her Patty. Patty started recognising the inmates of that building and started barking at the strangers /visitors. I gave Patty full attention and care; I knew Patty had already started proving her worth as my best companion and body guard.

Silver Salver.

Whenever an officer of our Regiment got married, it was customary to give a warm reception to the newly married couple at our officer's mess, at the earliest opportunity after their marriage and give them a special wedding gift. And if by chance the wife was unable to join the officer at the regimental location, the gift was then presented to the officer at a function organised at the officer's mess.

The wedding gift of his Regiment was a specially designed one - a beautiful six inches diameter silver salver, with the matter engraved in it, as 'Presented to (name of the Officer), by the Officers and their Families of (name of unit) Regiment, on (date, month and year). Further, it became more special with the signatures, of all officers held on the strength of the regiment on that date, engraved inside all around the main matter.

Thus, the wedding gift had an immense value as it was an expression of their love and affection towards you and it made you remember your good old days in the regiment.

In our case, this invaluable wedding gift was presented to me during a mess function organised at his Officer's mess at Pattan soon after we had reached Srinagar after our marriage, in early 1971.

There were twenty-one signatures engraved in our silver salver. And it was a token of their love and affection. We still recognise those signatures and their names even after a long spell of Forty-Nine years of our married life.

Celebration

First Wedding Anniversary.

April 27, 1971 was our first wedding anniversary. It was our desire to celebrate this special day at home with our parents, brothers, sisters and relatives; but we had come up to Srinagar only a couple of months earlier, in February and therefore, it was not possible for us to go down and celebrate this day at home. We felt a little bad and at home they knew that we were helpless. However, we decided to celebrate our first wedding anniversary in Srinagar.

We worked out a plan. We wanted to invite our officers and their families staying in Srinagar for a dinner at our home in Rajbagh, in Srinagar. This was going to be the first major event in our house. The day was falling on a week day, hence he requested for a short leave.

Organising such a big party meant a lot of preparation and we had just come to Srinagar. I did not any experience of arranging such a function. The expected crowd of about thirty, including our personal guests. Our flat had a limited space. It was still very cold in the evenings and we could not have arranged the party in our lawn below and so everything had to be arranged inside our house only. We earmarked our living room, one additional bed room and the hallway for the party.

Now, I was quite anxious to know as how to organise such a big party and also how we conducted the whole thing; obviously, I was the she was the lady of the house and everything would be counted, even how I conducted myself, herself during the party, from receiving the guests, engaging them during the party, entering into gossip with the ladies, talking to officers mainly answering their questions, serving good snacks and at the end, a good dinner, all mattered. My husband explained to me everything in detail so that it became easy for me to her to understand and get prepared for the situation.

When he finished explaining everything to me, I asked him, "But how do I communicate with such a crowd so well, to play a good host?"

He appreciated my concern. I was a double graduate and I had good knowledge in English and Hindi; but the only problem was fluency in these spoken languages. In Kerala, we always spoke our mother tongue, Malayalam. He had visualised this problem and therefore, after our marriage he had encouraged me in spoken English and Hindi to certain extent.

From April 1st 1971, I started teaching at the school. This coupled with her interaction with the landlord's daughters, had given her confidence in communicating both in English as well as in Hindi. But what I was worried about was, how do I interact with such a 'class crowd', at a party like this.

"There is nothing to worry about." In fact, he continued, you have improved a lot in your spoken languages more that he had expected from me. and that too within such a short span of time. I am really glad. He looked at me and gave a big smile. You will be able to do well at the party." I reassured her.

"I don't know.". Looking at him I replied. I wasn't sure.

We realised it wasn't so easy to organise such an event; we required help in cooking, crockery, cutlery, some linen, drinks and some mess staff. My husband formally invited his commanding Officer, our Commanding Officer, other officers including families of some of our officers staying in Srinagar. They welcomed our idea and were too glad to accept our invitation and assured us all possible help. His leave was sanctioned, without which we could not have arranged this party at all.

Great care was taken in planning; because we wanted everything to go very well, to be the best way possible, to make this as one of the memorable events in our life. We were organising such an event for the first time, and specially so for me, who did not have any such background in her life. We worked out an action plan. The rooms were thoroughly cleaned. We bought curtains for our windows. Whatever arrangements we needed from the mess were discussed with our Mess Secretary, who assured me everything including our mess staff. A special menu was selected in consultation with our mess cook.

A day earlier to our wedding anniversary, he came home on a short leave. We had to arrange our house and set the rooms for a lively party. After all it was in Srinagar, the world's paradise; flowers had started blooming and we wanted to fill the corners of our rooms with beautiful flower arrangements.

On the day of our wedding anniversary, we had a late morning and had our breakfast leisurely; it was a day for us to enjoy and was going to be a long day with our dinner party. The day was bright, clear and sunny. Our great friend, Patty was going to be three months old and had grown up. We made her realise that something was going to happen in our house in the evening and that she must get prepared for it. We planned to keep her in our bed room; she was quite understanding

.Arrangements for the Party
We then went to the city. We wanted to take our photo to mark the occasion and therefore, at a studio nearby, along the Bund Road we got ourselves photographed. It reminds us of our stay at Srinagar and those memorable moments we spent there. Oh! Everything was so beautiful. Later we bought flowers for the party.

My husband knew I like flowers very much. So, when we bought bunches of different flowers and carried them to our home, I was really happy, happy as ever, like those beautiful flowers. Since I loved flowers, I also had a liking for doing flower arrangements. he

Honeymoon Continues

Honeymoon continues in Kashmir.

It has become customary to plan a honeymoon to a place of your choice, for a short vocation, totally 'disconnected' from your contacts, undisturbed, and spend the whole time to yourself.

During the honeymoon days, the couples share their like and dislikes, dreams, understand each other, build their self-confidence and mutual trust. And all these exercises are supposed to strengthen your mutual relations and help you to make your married life very beautiful.

The location of your honeymoon, the place you chose to live, the duration your stay, all depended on your pocket size. Kashmir is one of the most sought after honeymoon locations in India and abroad.

When we got married on 27th April 1970, we also had planned a short honeymoon trip to Bangalore. Since he had to return to his Regiment, we could not extend our honeymoon days any longer. We had no regrets.

Now look at our destiny! Once again God has given us an opportunity to We are quite lucky to get such an opportunity where my husband posted to a located about 40 kilometres from Srinagar city. We also wanted to enjoy our second honeymoon, free of cost.

After reaching Kashmir in February 1971, my husband, Captain in the army, posted to a unit near

Pattan and I had teaching job at the prestigious Convent School in Srinagar. My husband used to come home to Srinagar on every weekend. What else you can hope for? The situation was very similar to the one we have our place in Kerala or for that matter anywhere in India. Hence, we wanted to stay in Kashmir as long as we can and enjoy our life.

We had a pleasant stay at Srinagar. It was lovely and lively. By now I learnt lot about army and army life. and started getting used to it. I really enjoyed my teaching job at the Presentation Convent Girls High School. At home, Patty really kept me busy and she was always a good companion to me. Srinagar city was compact and all areas were accessible.

The main mode of transport for local movement was *'Tanga'* and *'Shikkara'* to cross the channels. We visited almost all the places of tourist attraction in Kashmir, like Sri Sankaracharya temple, Dal lake, Char Chinar, Chashma Shahi, Shalimar, Pari Mahal, Wullar lake, Manasbal lake, Gulmarg, Pahalgam, Matton temple, Awanthipura ruins, Sona Marg, Amarnath Cave Shrine etc. It is difficult to describe the scenic beauty of the land. Anywhere you look it was just beautiful.

However, a few things are worth mentioning; like the time we used to spend hours in Shikkaras enjoying the beauty of Dal lake, walking up to the Sri Sankaracharya temple hill top and the aerial view of Dal lake with house boats all lined up. Oh! It was so magnificent! The gardens, Oh! they reflected the beauty of Kashmir - filled with full range of flowers, the colours, size, shape, fragrance, so beautiful they were. We used to spend the whole day in the gardens.

Kashmir valley had almost all fruits and flowers that are available in the western countries, due to its geographical location. There were different varieties of apple, apricot, strawberry, peaches, plum, mulberry, etc.

Dry fruits like almonds and walnut were also available. In addition, other fruits like mango, orange, pineapple, banana etc. were also available from other parts of the country. Whenever we used to go for on outings, fruits were major part of our food / refreshments. Oh! we really enjoyed the fruits.

A visit to some of the house boats gave us an idea as to why people preferred to stay in House Boats than in the luxurious hotels because the house boats were specially designed to cater the needs of the tourists; spacious, well laid out, well furnished, giving much personal care to the tourists, some of them even provided delicious food and to top it up they were very reasonably priced. Every one of them had a balcony in the front and terrace which provided the tourists a magnificent view of the Dal lake and the snow-covered mountain peaks. House boats were of different grades like hotels i.e. with 'star grading' one, two and three.

A Day in Dal Lake.

It was our long desire to spend a day Dal Lake one of the biggest lake sin Asia, I suppose. Once when my husband was home on a weekend, we decided to spend a few hours in dal lake alone. I still remember, it was a bright Sunday. We took a taxi and reached Dal Lake.

There were many vendors there selling flowers and all kinds of fruits. Kashmir being a well-known tourism spot even marked in the International Tourism Calendar, all types fruits were los available there.

You know, flowers and fruits are my weakness. I love them. We bought different varieties of fruits. Our landlord had told us about how to spend a day enjoying the beauty of Dal Lake. We anteed wanted to take a long ride in the Kashmiri Shikkara. My husband hired a Shikkara for about four hours and we moved in and settled down in the Shikkara.

As you can see the picture, it is a beautifully shaped well decorated where visitors can relax with a back rest.it was very comfortable. There was a one person in each Shikkara to take you wherever you want by using an ore.

The Shikkara fellow took us around all important places that were accessible along the water front. Oh! The Shikkara rid e was so enjoyable that during our stay in Srinagar we had a ride in Shikkara many a times.

Kashmir Is a garden of these beautiful flowers

Shikkara.

'Shikkara' was something like a small country boat, about twenty feet long with pointed ends on both ends. The middle portion was provided with a flat bed with proper backrest on one side of this bed so that at least two persons could relax on that. Now, this bed and the single seater had a canopy which was supported on four poles.

Shikkaras were generally well decorated with colourful cotton frills to make it more attractive. Each Shikkara had also a beautiful name. It required one person to paddle. The paddler sat on the end behind the back rest of the bed. I don't exactly remember how much we paid him; but the arrangement was that he would take us around various places of interests in Dal lake for about five hours and at the end he would leave us at the same spot from where we started our trip. We were all set to spend a beautiful day in the beautiful lake.

As we moved off, we passed by a number of house boats, some of the tourists/guests staying in house boats waving at us. It gave us a pleasant feeling, relaxing, eating fruits and moving against cool breeze. Everywhere it was looking so beautiful. Water in the lake was very clear. We could even see the weeds and plants that grew under water on the lake bed. There were a number of other tourists having a similar ride in Shikkaras. And we said hello to each other as we crossed, waving to each other. They were all tourists came to Kashmir for a short vacation.

I am enjoying a ride in a Shikkara. I
also se different type of Shikkaras.

House Boats.

Well decorated House Boats' added more beauty to the Dal Lake. A house Boat had a width of about 15 to 16 feet and length about fifty to sixty feet long floating structure. They had steps in the front to climb into from Shikkaras. These steps landed in the front veranda, wide enough for a few people to sit there and watch the lake. They always had a spacious sitting room, bedrooms and dining room and were all well-furnished. As in the case of hotels, they also had different grades; economy and luxury, luxury deluxe and so on. Some of them even had their star grading like one star, two star and three star and so on. Definitely it was worth staying a couple of days or even more in a house boat, as it was a unique experience; but it would all depend on your pocket size.

Each house boat had its own caretakers, who used to do everything possible for making your stay in the house boats most comfortable. They even used to provide food to their customers. Caretakers usually stayed in a separate small house boat behind the line of the main house boats. It was a wonderful sight to see the tourists staying in the house boats did their shopping from various vendors moving in Shikkaras loaded with stuff. You could find shikkaras carrying full of beautiful flowers, carrying delicious fruits of all varieties, Shikkaras carrying Kashmiri carpets which were very famous like Persian carpets, Shikkaras carrying clothing, handicraft items and other general items. They were really making a good

House Boats with their interior

business out there, perhaps more than the sale in some of the shops in the heart of the city.

Floating Gardens.

Floating gardens were another wondering phenomena in these lakes, especially in Dal lake. They were built over a period by creating/spreading layers of weeds and soil forming a floating media. And due to its buoyancy, it always floated on the water surface. The floating media had a few feet depth and an area as per their requirement; and this could be increased by creating more layers of weeds and thus increasing its buoyancy. On these floating gardens, people used to grow shallow routed vegetables flowers. These floating gardens were also movable within a limited area. Unbelievable! Isn't it? Well it is a fact. Whenever you get an opportunity to visit Srinagar and Dall lake, please don't miss to visit 'Floating Gardens'.

Char Chinar.

Another place of tourist attraction in Dal lake was 'Char Chinar'. It is Char Chinar only and not 'Char Minar' - an ancient monument and an important place of tourist attraction in Hyderabad in the state of Andhra Pradesh. This was a piece of ground, may be of size100 yards by 100 yards, I guess so, developed and protected from all around. Chinar is a beautiful tall tree with lots of branches; and had wide leaves. There were four Chinar trees there

On our return trip from Char Chinar we had a magnificent view of the lake in the fore front, the vast stretch of the road marking the boundary of the lake with the land, foot hills leading into high mountains on the left side, a partial view of the beautiful famous Shalimar and Chashma Shai gardens, Pari Mahal garden, Oberoi Palace Hotel complex and finally the Sankaracharya hill with its prominent Sankaracharya Temple on top.

Below given are three pictures of Char Chinar, I have been talking about. Since we had reached Kashmir, during February 1971 Winter had already set in and the trees had already shed their leaves. They were looking like their skeleton. Now they had to wait until Spring comes back once again smiling, for their leaves to grow. This would make them all look very beautiful once again. They would then would welcome the world to Kashmir, the 'Paradis' on Earth.

Roads with Poplar trees during Winter

Char Chinar during Winter, Spring and During Autmn

At Shankaracharya Temple

6

Gulmarg -An International Tourist Destination

It was our desire to visit to most of the famous tourist destinations in Kashmir as far as possible. And we jointly had made a list of such places. Gulmarg was one of the internationally known tourist stations in Kashmir. So, we decided to visit Gulmarg during one of the weekends. It was a small valley by itself within the big valley; surrounded by big mountains like Killan Marg on one side and by high hills on the other sides. It was about just over 1hour drive from Srinagar.

Gulmarg is located above 9,000 ft. above the mean sea level. During winter, Gulmarg and the areas around got very heavy snow fall and it stayed little longer than any other such places in the valley. We had gone there sometime during June, by then, snow along the road and on the sides had melted away. Barring a few patches of snow on the hill slopes, snow had totally vanished. A clear blue sky with a few patches of snow-white clouds welcomed us to the small valley. It was bright and sunny.

The valley looked beautiful with undulating gentle slopes coming down into the valley. It looked as if the beautiful valley was being guarded by the mountains and high hills all around. The main road entering the valley continued further through the centre of the valley to the other end of the valley and climbed up the mountain for the defence requirements. We found beautiful huts put up along the inside perimeter of the valley, tucked into the woods, meant for hiring out to the tourists. There were also a few big hotels, to cater to the needs of the tourists. In the centre of the valley was the prestigious Gulmarg Golf Club.

Gulmarg during summer

Gulmarg during Spring and Winter

Amarnath Cave Shrine

A pilgrimage spot over 12,000 feet

An important event during our stay in Kashmir was our visit to the famous pilgrimage spot 'Amarnath Cave Shrine' situated in the Himalayas in south Kashmir. The pilgrimage to this famous Amarnath Cave Shrine always began sometime during the month of July; and the Shrine was kept open for the 'Darshan' for a short period due to the weather conditions.

Generally, we had only weekends for our pleasure trips, we used to take full advantage of weekends and holidays. And at times, a couple of days leave gave us more room. Thus once, we along with another officer and his family planned to visit this famous pilgrimage spot.

There were two routes to this place; first one was the traditional route - from Srinagar via Pahalgam, Chandanwari, Sheshnag, Panjtarni, Sangam and on to the cave shrine. This was a mule track. The distance was so much that it required three to four days for a return trip; and therefore, the state government had made arrangements for tented accommodation and other facilities including medical and protection, en route at some important places. The state government always opened this route for the tourists in the season.

The second route was from Srinagar to Sonamarg

and to Baltal and from there, along the newly built mule track to Sangam and on to the cave shrine. This route though short, involved traversing more heights and difficult areas; but one could make the journey from Sonamarg to Amarnath cave and back in one day. And we decided to take this route.

We don't really remember the date; but it was sometime in August 1971, on a clear day, we started our journey to Amarnath cave via Sonamarg and Baltal. From Srinagar to Sonamarg, we went by the state transport bus and reached there in the afternoon. Our overnight stay at Sonamarg was already arranged with the 'High Altitude Warfare School' (HAWS), there. At the Sonamarg Tourist centre we met the Head of the Himalayan Mountaineering Institute, along with his wife; they were also planning to visit Amarnath cave shrine on the next day.

Sonamarg was pretty cold in the night. Next day, we were to start early. HAWS authorities were kind enough to provide us with a vehicle for going up to Baltal. We reached Baltal by about 7.30 or so; and from there we had to go either on foot or on a pony. So, he hired a pony for me and my husband decided to walk. Other family also did the same. We had carried our pack lunch, some fruits and drinking water.

We started moving along the mule track; it was a narrow track where only one mule (load carrying animal looking like little bigger than a horse) could comfortably walk. And any crossing/over taking had to be done very carefully. We were moving at comfortable speed. To give an idea of the route, we were moving on a mule track with steep mountains on one side and deep gorges on the other side.

The sight all around gave a panoramic view of high mountains with white patches of snow- and snow-covered peeks, with some springs flowing down the valley. But we could not really enjoy these views always, because, any loss of concentration on our part, had a chance of falling into the gorges below. En route, we stopped at places for rest and refreshments we had carried.

Much before noon we reached a place called Sangam, the meeting point of both the routes, i.e. via Baltal and via Pehalgam to Amarnath cave shrine. From there it was a few kilometres to the cave further climbing up the mountain.

We are on our way to Amarnath Cave Shrine

In the background do you see snow coverd mountains with steep slops.? The mule tracj was just boeut 6 to 8 fret wide. And if the mule make ny extra rdinary moves ,you had it it was so risky.

Amarnath Cave Shrine

Snow Bridge.

Have you heard of 'Snow Bridge'? During winter the whole area was covered under heavy snow specially hundreds of feet of snow in the gorges. In the Spring, the snow starts melting and by summer almost all the snow in the valley in these areas gets melted away. However, there shall be patches where sun rays don't fall at all or fall partially. In these areas, heavy snow beds remain.

During summer, since the temperature of the soil is more than the melting temperature of ice, the snow in contact with soil gets melted away. And gradually as the temperature builds up, snow much above the ground also gets melted away, thus forming a cave sort of thing at places and water flows underneath. When this kind of thing comes en route, people walk over this and this acts as a bridge which is stronger and stays till it collapses after a period of time, after more snow melted away. Thus, during our journey we crossed over a couple of such snow bridges. Finally, we reached a point from where we got a beautiful distant view of Amarnath Cave Shrine.

It was time for lunch; we had our lunch; there was a small spring flowing nearby; water was crystal clear, and very cold. We drank from it, freshened ourselves and rested a while. Before we began our journey from there, he took some pictures with Amarnath Cave Shrine in the back ground. It was located at a height over 12,000 ft.

We took another twenty to thirty minutes to reach the mouth of the cave. The cave was quite big. There were a number of other devotees offering their prayer. The 'Chari Mubarak' (holy mace) was always taken by the Sadhus from Srinagar as per the tradition and lead the first main yatra. A few Sadhus were also seen chanting some 'manthras'. 'Shivalingam' was the idol at this cave and this 'Shivalingam' was of hard snow which was quite tall during winter and short during summer days, obviously snow was melting away. We also saw few white doves flying around and having their nests there. It is believed, we were told, that those were the 'athmas'/spirit of the holy men, who had laid their lives there.

We stayed there for some time watching the beauty of the land; had our refreshments, freshened ourselves again with the clean cold stream water and started our journey back. On our return, we followed the same route.

Coming down was more difficult than going up, specially sitting on a pony. By evening we reached back Baltal from where an army vehicle from HAWS had come to take us to Sonamarg. The journey was quite tiring; because, even sitting on a mule/ pony for such a long journey was also quite tiring. Again, we stayed the night at the HAWS officers mess at Sonamarg. Next day morning we returned to Srinagar by bus. It was indeed a memorable journey.

Thus, we didn't really know when winter turned to spring, spring turned to summer and summer turned to autumn, till we started seeing the leaves of Chinar trees turning into yellow and orange and the leaves started falling. We could see a total colour change in the valley; it was so beautiful to look at. Thus, though we had only the weekends and few holidays, we had really enjoyed our stay together at Srinagar, more than perhaps one could think of.

Srinagr gardens looks very to colourful with Trees cahnging the color of their leaves.(Below; at Char Chinnar, you find the four chinar tees whicth during the color changing activities her.

At L o C with Pakistan

Visit to L o C in Uri Sector.

During his weekend visit, my husband asked me, "Dear, since a few officers of our regiment have their family staying in Srinagar, our CO was planning to take officers and their families to LoC in Uri sector. Are you interested? Shall we go?"

When he finished talking, immediately I said, "Of course I want go, we will go ok?"

"Yes, of course we will go. Happy? And we both had a laugh.

Sometime later, on a weekend, we along with a few others and their families went to visit the LoC Uri Sector. My husband had briefed me about the details the visit. I was little scared since we were going to a place very close to our enemy. But he asked me not to worry." Nothing will happen. We are going there to one such border posts our country has with Pakistan. We have obtained necessary permission to visit the area.

Before our country was partitioned, there was a road connecting Srinagar and Rawalpindi, now in Pakistan. The road from Srinagar passed through Pattan, Baramulla, Rampur, Uri and onward through other places in Pakistan and finally to Rawalpindi. The international border between India and Pakistan now ran across this main road at a place ahead of a place called 'Weak Bridge'. Our border post at this location was called 'Kaman Post'.

Similarly, a border post was also set up by Pakistan across the border on their side. These border out posts were very important; because, very often the United Nations Observer Staff used this axis to go to Rawalpindi and vice versa. Moreover, this axis was also used for the movement of senior officers across, for their 'Flag Meetings' in this sector.

Uri was about 66 kilometres away from Srinagar; and this particular post was about 20 to 25 kilometres further away along the same road axis. It was about an hour and a half drive from my husband's regiment location. unit location. After Baramulla, the road was going along the banks of the famous river Jellum. As we were nearing Rampur, we saw a huge construction site where an important hydel project was under construction. Soon we reached Uri township. It had a small wayside market, with dwelling on both sides of the road on the upper and lower reaches.

From Uri, we proceeded further till we were stopped at a place called 'Red Bridge' for traffic checking. In a literal sense, there was an iron girder bridge (a type of bridge construction), painted in red. There, they checked our documents and allowed us to go further. We were nearing our destination. Ladies were all excited, after all, they were nearing the international border between India and Pakistan. For each one of them it was going to be their first and a rare experience in their lives.

After a few kilometres we reached a place called 'Weak Bridge'. This was again another bridge and as the name suggested this bridge was really weak and allowed only light vehicles to go over this bridge. There again our documents were checked and allowed us to proceed further with a caution, that we should go very slowly. As directed, we went further and within minutes, we reached a sign board where it was written - 'No vehicles beyond this point'. Another one said 'Report here'.

We parked our vehicle in the parking area along the side of the road and reported to the sentry on duty. They were all in their 'battle dress' carrying their loaded personal weapons. Before starting, we had informed the unit headquarters who was in charge of this 'Kaman Post' of our proposed visit; and we being the Divisional Engineers, always got a cordial welcome wherever we went. Hence, they knew that we were coming there for a visit. The sentry on duty in their intercom informed their local commander of our arrival.

Immediately their local commander came to the spot and welcomed us to their prestigious border out post. He took us through their covered underground communication trenches to various observation bunkers and explained and showed us the Pakistani border out post across, which was only about less than a hundred yards away. Through the binoculars we saw clearly the Pakistani soldiers moving at their location in kakhi uniform carrying their personal weapons. They had seen a vehicle approaching towards the 'Kaman Post' and therefore, their sentries on duty were quite vigil and observing at our Post.

The Post Commander offered us tea in mugs, in the traditional way and some snacks. We thanked them for their hospitality and started our return journey.

The ladies were very much excited over the fact they were able to visit and experience one of the important Border Out Posts (BOP) between our country India and Pakistan on the actual Line of Control (LoC). Certainly, this visit was one of the most exciting and memorable events in my life. Thanks to my husband.

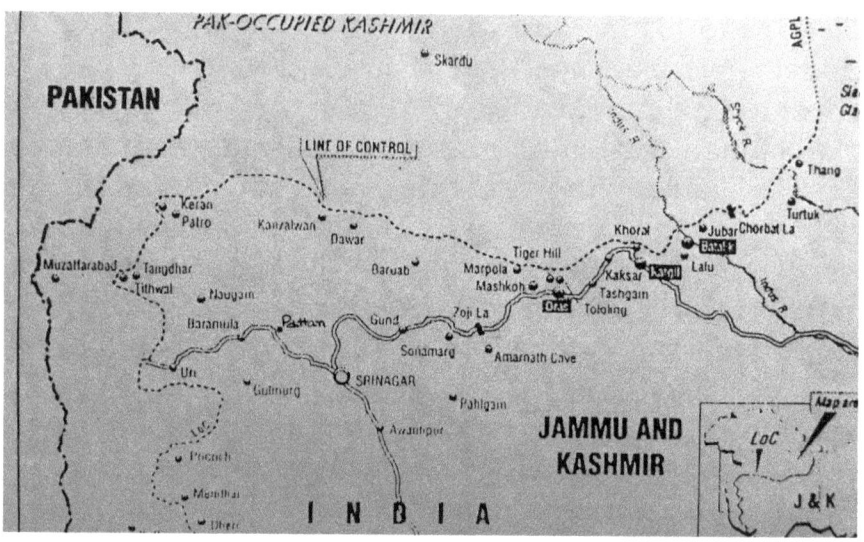

This is a map showing National Highway, after Srinagar, bifurcates int o two; one going to teh eastern direction to placeda like Snnamarg, Kargil sectors nd yhe othe r ones goes via Pattan and Baramulla to Uri, to the Lo C wtih Pakistn.

Scary Days of My Life

1971 Indo-Pak War

1971 Indo-Pak War was most memorable and unforgettable event in my life. During this period, there were moments of joy and sorrow, good and bad times, and moments of worry and tension.

It was our joint decision to be always together after our marriage. Accordingly, I had resigned my teaching job and joined my husband. And now, here is a situation, where we are compelled to live separately. My husband could have managed himself; because he was staying with his regiment. Whereas, here at Srinagar, I was all alone in a three storied house with my puppy, Patty. There was no one to talk to, no contact with my husband, a total silence everywhere. I could hear Air attack warning alarms, power cuts. Oh, it was a total confusion. At times negative thought drove me off the track and took me to the 'dead end'. But it was our Dream about a beautiful family life with our children that brought me back to positive thoughts.
"I would prefer to stay near my husband in Srinagar than going to my home in Kerala and live with my parents", I told my husband.

Everything was going very well. You know Kashmir with its fruits, flowers and the landscaping is known as the paradise of the world. And we wanted to enjoy as much as we could. In a way, it was our extended period of honeymoon.

On one weekend when my husband came home, I found him little tensed. So, I asked him, 'Why are you looking tensed?' any problem?

'Nothing, he said. I was not happy his answer. Because I have known him for a few years and I could read his face. I knew something was wrong somewhere. I told him, 'I know there is something is disturbing you, please tell me or else, I will start worrying about you.' I told him.

'Leela', he called me in a soft tone. It sounded his concern for me. He continued, 'You know, the relationship between our country and Pakistan is not really in good terms. In the recent months tension has been building up all along the Indo Pak Border. It doesn't look like the situation will be diluted. Our formation in this sector is all prepared to take on any surprise moves by Pakistan.

So, as a precautionary measure, our Regiment has received instruction to give the addresses and details of our families staying at Srinagar and requested the units to plan despatch of their families to their homes. Everybody started sending their families back. Officers and other ranks from our regiment who had their families, have also been asked to despatch their families back home. I was trying to continue my dialogue.

I knew what he was going to tell me. Before he started, I told him, **"I would prefer to stay near my husband in Srinagar than going to my home in Kerala and live with my parents".**

He told me all the consequences of staying back during this period of uncertainty and the risks involved; and tried to persuade me to go home. But I refused to accept my suggestion. I told him, "I understand what you are saying; but I would prefer to stay near my husband in Srinagar rather than going to my home in Kerala and live with my parents."

Finally, he conceded my request. But we had a hard time in convincing our parents. Later he gave my address and other particulars to his unit authorities to keep a track of my safety and extend any help to me in case of an emergency.

I used to listen to the radio news, both Indian news as well as the Pakistani radio. There were reports of border violations, firing across the border at a number of places and Pakistani aircrafts entering our air space. All these activities normally did not happen in a peacetime condition. Everyone felt something was going happen.

The situation further deteriorated. Anything could happen at any time. My husband used to come home on weekends as usual. That was great relief for me.

Pain of Separation
He told me in case the situation worsens further, then he said he may not be able to come home; but he assured me not to worry, everything will be taken care of. He also explained to me if the situation goes beyond control, it could lead into an aggression between India and Pakistan.

married. After we were married, we always wanted to be together. And never wanted to be separated. But look at the situation, how could I bear the pain of separation?

After a while my husband said good bye and returned to his regiment. I couldn't control myself. I felt as if I have lost everything and I am all alone in the world. Immediately after he left, I closed the doors of the house including the ground floor door, came up to our bedroom and I let it out. But after a while, I regained control over myself and mentally and physically. I thought of my husband and his words, which made me stronger.

Daily I used to listen to the new bulletin of both India and Pakistan. My student living nearby uses to come to me and I used to go their place occasionally. There were no Cell phones in those days. And it was little difficult to communicate from an army unit to a civil telephone no in Srinagar city. But My husband had told me, if anything urgent, he will certainly send some messenger with a note to me.

As he had told me, after a few days, one messenger from his regiment came to our house and gave me a cover form my husband. The situation was getting bad to worse. So, I could not have expected anything better. Anyway, I opened the cover and read the content. It said. 'Hello my dear Leela, as you must have heard for the news bulletin, the situation is going bad to worse, anything could happen at any

I was little afraid. Because, the Major and his wife staying on the ground floor had already left .so the ground floor was empty. The land lord's family staying on the second floor also had let for Delhi to their relative's place. And I was all alone that big house, if anything happens to me no one will come to know.

I became very tensed, which my husband noticed. But he never mentioned to about my decision to stay back in Srinagar was wrong. Instead, he told me, "You could have gone home. Several time I had requested you to consider going home. But you never agreed to it. Instead, what he did was, he hugged tight, kissed me and told me, "Don't you worry about anything, dear. It is your love for me that you took the decision to stay back. I really appreciate your guts to stay back alone in this hose. God is with us. He will take care of us."

It was already Sunday evening, and he had to return to his regiment. We both were helpless. But we knew we have to be bold and face the situation. One of my students was living very near to our house. So, I could go to them anytime. We bid goodbye to each other. His regiment vehicle was waiting for him to return to his unit. And he left to his Regiment.

The situation was such very seldom others could understand. We had loved each other and it was our desire to get married. By God's blessing everything went well, with the blessing of our parents we got time.   Further movement of personnel is also restricted. Hence, I won't be coming home until the situation improves. Let us hope for the best. Take care Bye. And he kissed me. I didn't know how to react. Somehow, I controlled myself wrote a note to my husband about what's happening here and gave it to the messenger. It was December 01 1971.

We didn't have to wait for long, on December03, Both the countries, India and Pakistan declared War against each other.

Great relief to my turbulent mind

The war continued. After the war started, I noticed that movements in our neighbourhood had almost stopped. Hardly I saw anyone on the road. Sometime I used to get scared. For my food, we had kept enough stock at home. And for any additional help I could tell Shahitha, my student who was living nearby. In fact, she used to come to me daily and spend and returned to her home. That was the only contact I had. And of course, Patty our pet dog, she was my companion, and my security guard.

One day as usual all alone in our house, I was listening to the new bulletin on the radio news. It must be around lunch time. I heard some knocking the ground floor entrance door. I came to our sit out and looked I was surprised. My husband was standing outside the entrance door. For a moment, I lost my sense. I asked myself, how is he here? Anyway, I was so happy to see him, I went opened the door. It was about three weeks ago he had come home. After that everything was uncertain. But it was like our reunion after many years. We hugged each other.

My husband's visit was totally unexpected; and when I saw him, I burst into tears; I had seen him much before the war started and we were meeting after a few weeks. Pakistan's false propaganda about the bombing and destruction of units at Pattan had caused further confusion and fear; after all, I was staying there all alone with our pet Patty giving company to me. My happiness found no bounds. We had a lot of things to talk. I was very anxious to know about, how come he was here? what was his pan etc.

"So', Before I started, he began.

"You see my dear, there is total restriction on personnel movements within our Divisional area and outside. Our Commanding Officer knows, you are the only family from our regiment staying back in Srinagar. He also knows that it has been a few weeks after I last visited you. So, he called me to his office, and asked me, Captain George, the war will continue and everything will go on; but we know, your wife is saying back in Srinagar, and she is alone in the house. So, don't you worry, I have obtained a special permission from or GOC of our formation." He continued,

"This is a special a permission for you to travel up to Srinagar, and get some work done at the FOD (Field Ordinance Depot). But you just go to the FOD, enter your name in the arrival register and after sometime you also enter the out time and after that I want you to go to your wife, spend a few hours with her and come back in the evening. And if anyone ask you for the details, you just show them the travel permission.

That's all. Ok all the best."

"That's how I am here. Got it." He said he had to go back around 4 p.m.

"I am so happy to see you." I told him

"Now, tell me about you, what is the news. You were to go to school in December first week No? What happened? Could you go?"

'Yes'. "You know, our school was closed on December 01st and we were to give the 'results' to the school on December 03rd", I said.

"How did you go?", he asked.

"Ms. Khurana had come in her car and we both went to the school, gave the 'results' and she dropped me back home. As I got out of the car, we heard siren, which was a warning of an air attack, as we were told by the army security personnel. So, Ms. Khurana also came inside the house. We heard sound of fighter aircrafts flying over Srinagar city. After sometime, we heard another siren, which marked the end of an air threat." She continued, "Really I got a shock of my life. After Ms. Khurana left, I listened to the news in the radio, both Indian and Pakistan, the war had begun. Since then, I had sleepless nights. I always listened to the news in the radio."

Then he told me about the air attack, their air strikes.

It said about air attacks, bombings, and fighting along the border in various sectors. All the time I was worried about you."

"Leela, that was why I had told you in the beginning itself to go home, so that you could feel more comfortable with our parents." He said.

But I could not accept his view point. Immediately I asked him, "How could I be comfortable there? Here, at least I know what is going on; and there, I would not have come to know about anything until everything was over and I got a letter from you. I would have been more worried there." She was very much concerned about me.

He interrupted, 'I am sorry I didn't mean to hurt you.'

I continued, "Here, everyday seemed to be the longest day of my life. In spite of all this, I tried to control myself and regain my mental strength. But one day, the morning news I heard that Pakistan aircrafts had bombed over the army units at Pattan and caused very casualties really upset me."

"I can understand. That's why I spoke to you that day over the telephone." he said.

"It was only when you spoke to me that I had a sigh of relief. But, from the moment I heard the radio news, till I heard your voice over the phone, only I knew, the mental agony I went through." As I said this, tears started coming out of my eyes. And I couldn't control myself. My husband held me tight.

After a long pause I continued, "All kinds of thoughts came to my mind. I didn't feel like doing anything. I sat in our bedroom and started praying, that you should be safe and nothing should happen to you. It was then, some of my colleagues, teaching at the Presentation Convent school, came home. They wanted to know about my welfare and we had some casual discussion. I knew, they couldn't change my destiny and therefore, I didn't tell them about the Pakistan radio news I heard, till I myself was sure of it. They also didn't mention anything about it to me. They probably would have thought that I was not aware of that news and why to make me worry.

After sometime they left. I was sure to get some message from you from Pattan. It was then Ms Shahida, my student, and her father came to me and told that there was a phone call from you from Pattan and that you wanted to speak to me. I went with them to their house. After sometime your call came; I was so happy to hear your voice. They accompanied me back home. I thanked God for everything."

I wanted to let him know everything that happened during these days. "You know dear", I continued, "Soon after the war started, the army security personnel had come again and told me to be more careful about the safety aspects and also said that there was no point in writing letters as there would not be any movement of mail up and down. From December 03rd onwards, every day I used to hear siren, which was a warning for an air attack and again another one to mark the end of such a threat. *On some days, there used to be such warnings for more than one air attack. Initial days, I was quite scared and whenever I heard a siren, I used to close all doors and windows and remain inside the house. Later, I gained confidence and on hearing such warnings, I used to watch outside in the sky from our sit out. Once I saw two aircrafts flying over Srinagar city, chasing each other; Oh! It was an exciting sight."*

"Well, you already have enough of war experience, don't you?", he smiled at me.

And I returned the smile; and asked him, "Can I come and stay with you at Pattan?

"No chance. You see, no countries in the world can afford to fight a prolonged war. So definitely it will come to an end soon. Let us hope that the worst is over. Take care of yourself. Everything is going to be alright." He consoled me.

My husband's unexpected visit had given me great relief to my turbulent mind and helped me to me to regain my self-confidence to stay alone and face any situation. After spending some more time together, he returned to his unit. We thanked hia Commanding Officer for his good gesture.

War Ends: India and Pakistan accept Cease Fire.

Mounting world pressure were compelling both India and Pakistan to call for a cease fire. Finally, Cease Fire was declared on December 17,1971. Though all major actions across the international border were called off, it took some time to come back to normalcy. It was my sheer mental strength I had that I could absorb the shock of events, according to my husband. He really admired my strength and courage, even our regimental officers congratulated me for this brave act. The situation cooled down.

At our homes in Kerala, they were really worried; but couldn't really do much except to pray to God Almighty to take care of their children. After the war was over, we wrote to them detailed letters.

After the Cease Fire was declared and accepted by both the countries, the situation along the Indo-Pak border gradually returned to normalcy. My husband came home for Christmas. We celebrated our X' mas at Srinagar. However, this being a post war winter no one could really enjoy it. It had snowed heavily during that winter.

SSB for Permanent Commission

My Husband had joined the army as a Shor Service Commission, SSC (NT- 3), for a period of Five years from August 1967 to August 1972 So it was time for his selection for permanent commission. As per the instructions he was to report to the SSB at Jabalpur during February/ March 1972.

Due to severe winter and heavy snow fall, all the roads were blocked/ closed and there was no flights also. It was a really a situation where you could not do anything. A couple of times hoping there would be flights he had gone to the Srinagar airport only to have come back disappointed. We both became very tensed. If did not make it on the date to SSB he would have lost his chance to get his permanent commission.

Finally, on the last day he was to leave to reach the SSB on time luckily there was a flight from Delhi. He got ready and said bye to me. We didn't know what would happen, I wished him best of Luck and told him,' don't worry, this time everything is going to be alright. And he left for the airport. And I kept my fingers crossed. And started praying to god to help him.

After a few hours, he called me from the airport. He said, there was a flight, but a small air craft. It was almost very difficult o get in, but the pilots realised the seriousness of my situation and so he called me to come up at the last minute before closing the door of the aircraft. Rest I shall tell you on my return Ok." I was so happy I thanked prayed that he should get he should also be selected for the permanent commission.

He was almost away for nearly 10 days. Heavy snow falls continued. But this time I was not alone in the house. Landlord and his family had returned from Delhi. After the SSB selection was over, he called me from Jabalpur that he was selected and everything was fine. I congratulated him. It was yet another tense situation which each one of you will understand.

Spring Smiles Again

Spring came smiling again. It was brighter, brighter than last year, may be because it had an added pleasant air of victory. Everybody seemed to be more enthusiastic. And we were feeling on top of the world. Specially we had great reasons for joy; I was pregnant and he was going to become a father.

The schools reopened; and I started teaching again. Our parents were very anxious to see us after the war. And this 'Great News' made them happy and more anxious. Thus, we decided to go on my annual leave in May 1972.

Srinagar to Kerala

We repeated our good old journey from Srinagar back to Thrissur. But this time our pet Patty was fully grown up and we had great bundles of golden memories of our life in Srinagar. Further, I had a special news, I was pregnant. We were also very anxious to meet our parents and dear ones.

After about five days long journey, we reached our home. They were all very happy to see us back home. In fact, I was given a hero's welcome as if I had fought the Indo - Pak war. I had a lot to things to share with everyone at home and to my friends, for days together; even our pet dog Patty also had lot of things to share.

Our Life in Kashmir - Days makede us stronger both physically and mentally

Since my husband had come on his annual leave, we were together and we visited our relatives and friends. And they were all very happy to see us back home. In fact, they were all quite surprised how could I get the courage and mental strength to face such a situation.

Our lifestay in Kashmir, gave me good exposure life and traught me how to face the challenges of the outside world. It also helped us to understand and learn more about each other, which drew us more closer. We also learned a lot more, which came as a great help in our later life.

It also gave us lot of opportunities to learn about different culture, especially about life in the army which I consider was the most valuable experience which helped me to be a successful wife, a mother and to be a good host in li life. Further, we realised, it is the mutual trust and mutual support that make your make your relationship better and make our life more beautiful.

After his leave, he left me home for my delivery and he returned all the way back to join my regiment at the same old location. This time he was all alone; but then he had lots of unforgettable memories to carry with him. We knew it was going to be very difficult for us to live separately. Especially so, our memories of our exciting and emotional experience we lived through in the recent months were still fresh in our minds that I always felt his presence around me. I am sure he would have felt the same. I made it a point to write to him regularly, even he wrote to me very often. We never waited for a one to one reply; often our letters were replies for some previous ones.

Normally it took minimum a week for his letters to reach me and another week for my letters to reach him; thus, it took a fortnight to get a reply to our letters from the date we posted our letters. It was quite a long wait; and we could not afford to wait that much. We wanted a letter from our sweet heart after every few days.

So, we wrote a letter after every two to three days, without waiting for a reply; in these letters we referred to the points of her/my earlier points. Thus, we were almost getting one or two letters in a week. These letters were our strength to live, even being away from each other. Oh! those were the days.

Becoming Proud Parents
On September 23, 1972I gave birth to a baby girl. By Ggod's blessing everything was ok. We informed him about the good news. And he too was quite thrilled. He wanted to come for a short break to visit us. Bbut unfortunately, his regiment was under the orders of move to another location, so he could not make it. We felt very bad.

After a few months he came home. We both were so happy to see each other after a few months. I felt very proud to be the mother of our baby girl. When I gave her. He took her in her arms kissed he our daughter and held her close to his chest and looked and d smiled at me. We have become the proud parents.

We thanked God for our baby girl. After spending a few days, together, he returned to his unit. and returned to his unit at the new location. During his visit he mentioned that he had been detailed for doing the engineering degree at CME from May 1973. I and our daughter planned to join him at CME after May 1973.

Engineering Degree at Government's expense?
My husband's ambition was to become an Engineer. and join the Corps of Engineers of the Indian Army. But, during his Pre- University Course examination days, he was down with 'Chicken Pox'. With great difficulty he had managed to write the exams; towards the end, he became so weak that he couldn't write my last exam. Due to this, he could not get admission to the engineering college; he felt bad. He joined for a bachelor's degree, B.Sc. in Maths.

Since he had lost the chance to become an engineer, he took more interest in the National Cadet Corps (NCC); he wanted become an officer in the army. He was lucky. He got selected for the Short Service Commission for 5 years in the army. I decided to join the Corps of Engineers.

Now, after five years of service, he was granted permanent commission and was detailed to attend the Engineering Degree Course at the College of Military Engineering (CME) at Dapodi near Pune. It was a 3- year degree course from May '73 to May '76, affiliated to the Pune University. Look at his luck! He could take a bachelor's degree B.Sc., He had become an officer in the army and now, he was going to do my engineering degree. I was so happy; it was all God's blessing.

Life at CME.

Life at CME was entirely different. It was a self-contained campus. It was mostly a student life. Morning physical training, attending classes, evening games and doing project work etc. We had a comfortable family life. I learned cycling there. Weather was quite pleasant in Pune.

We managed to get another pup, this time it was a Lhasa Apsoo. It was again a bitch, belonged to small variety. We named her as Dimple. My daughter had already developed an interest with our earlier pet, Patty whom we had left behind at Thrissur. And now she had a liking for pets; she loved Dimple so much that given permission she loved to keep Dimple in her bed.

While at CME I conceived my second child. Since we were alone in Pune, my mother from home came to help us. I was hospitalised at the military hospital in pune. Everything was ok. On November 27, 1975, I give birth to a baby boy. Everybody was happy. His degree course would be over in May 1976. Our life at CME was very comfortable.

As his Degree Course was getting over, he received his posing order. We were quite surprised. He has been posted to his old Regiment and at the same old location. The only difference, the good news attached to families were also allowed at his unit location in a restricted way. In the sense there were no proper permanent accommodation for the families, only, whereas the units provided some kind of adhoc arrangements for their families.

X'Mas Celebrations

Family Holidaying

Back to Kashmir

Back to Kashmir

After the engineering degree course, from CME Pune he was posted to his old Regiment. It was at the same old location near Pattan which was about 40 km from Srinagar towards Baramulla. After availing the joining time, we moved to the new location at Pattan. From Pune to Bombay, to Delhi, to Jammu, to Udhampur to Srinagar and to Pattan. During his earlier tenure in the Regiment, only I was there, staying at Srinagar; whereas now, we were moving as family with all household things including our motor bike. This time we left our new pet Dimple at our home.

Some of our other officers also had their families at Pattan. Hence, it was a very small family station; a new experience to them. No cooking, food used to come from our mess. Some of the families had school going children, even our daughter was getting ready to go to Kindergarten. The only school available was the famous St. Joseph's High School at Baramulla, near the Divisional headquarters, about 18 kms from our location. It was run by the priests. There was a convent, church and a hospital too, near this school. Later, our daughter was admitted in that school at Baramulla in UKG. Our life was progressing and our family started growing.

Our stay at Pattan was really comfortable and enjoyable. There were about 6 to 8 families from our own regiment were there. Some of them had school going children. The living s arrangements were little restricted that was the only minus point. Children were admitted to the St. Joseph's High School at Baramulla. Some vehicle used to drop them at the school and pick them up after their classes. And after they returned from their classes, they used to play together.

Now, as far as wives of the officers, some time we used to address them as lady officer. They were really enjoying their life. No cooking. we used to get our food from their Officer's mess. And their children once gone to school, in the morning, they would come back, in the evening. Their husbands, officers were always busy with their unit affairs. Thus, the ladies of our regiment were mainly utilised their time for gossiping and also for sharing the knowledge on some like, knitting, tatting, stitching embroidery, then sharing of some cooking lessons etc.

On holidays/ weekends each famly or a few families together used to plan some activities or organise some functions at the mess all officers and their families and their children had fully participated in such programmes

Another main advantage of such stay was that, it was also a meeting point for different culture from across our Country India. And this included the different languages, social culture, social customs including their food habits and all. Thus, the ladies enjoyed and learnt a lot more. At time we used to walk across the apple orchids nearby, looking at the way apple growing on the trees, and we used to pluck apples form the apple trees. Oh! We could not have wished of a better life than this.

At Pattan we were there from May 1976 to December 1978. That means, three Springs and three Winters. Another long holidays for our family in Kashmir. I cannot forget the life experience I have had at Pattan when living with our children.

Our winter at Pattan

Feeling Great – Family together in winter

Our children really enjoyed their stay at Pattan during winter.

Life at Other Stations

Kashmir to Vizag

After about two and half years my husband was posted from Kashmir to Vizag, to a unit, under CEDD, A special organisation Responsible of the design and construction of the Dry Dock. for the Indian navy. Oh! It was a Mega Project. At Vizag our children went to school. military organization known as Military Engineering Service MES our daughter was admitted at the central School and son was admitted to. LKG. My husband had a quite a busy with his work and life there, where as we had a routine life there. At vizag also we visited some places of interest like, Dolphin Nose, Vizag Beach,

At Vizag, my husband started playing Golf, very expensive game. Only a few in the army played this game. I supported his interest. He bought a Golf half set from their defence canteen. Golf course was at 10 to 12 kilometres away. He used to play golf with some senior officers there. They all used to go together in a car, paly their game of golf at the Vizag Golf Club and come back around 6 p.m. And during this duration, we were alone at home. But I knew how much he did for us. So, I valued his personal interest and we gave him our full support.

We must have stayed for about two years plus after that my husband was posted back to his old regiment near Calcutta, but this time on promotion to the rank

At Vizag Beach

Teaching them reading habit

Vizag to Calcutta

Soo after reporting to his unit, he was promoted to the rank of a Major. My husband's Regiment was near Calcutta for nearly four years and it was expecting it's move orders anytime to another location and as expected the move orders was received to move from the present location to Sikkim. Being a peace location, we, my husband, our two children and me were staying at the officer's quarters near our regiment.

My husband was detailed as the OIC Advance party, to take a team of officers, JCOs and men, go to the new location and to start taking over so that the Regiment could move accordingly. to the new location. I and our two children stayed back and my husband along with his team went to Sikkim.

In the meantime, my husband's posting also came to some Military Engineering Service (MES) unit at Wellington, in Nilgiris Dist. We were so happy that finally we were moving to a place, which was at only a few hours' drive from our home town.

On a Sunday morning at our officer's mess

Our family - in front of our quarters at Calcutta

Moving to Sikkim

It was his desire to take us to Sikkim for a few days, just for sightseeing, before he moved out of his regiment. Permission was granted. The planning was, they would travel from Calcutta to NJP by train (AC coach); and from there, on the same day, travel by officer's bus to Gangtok, where he would meet us. Everything wen as per our plan he met us at Gangtok Transit Camp; from where he came and picked us. In spite of their long tiring journey, we feeling very happy to be there with me, in Sikkim, for a short and sweet pleasure cum sight-seeing trip.

In Sikkim, we stayed with our unit at Five Mile, as no families were permitted beyond that point in East Sikkim. We had only a few days with us and wanted to make full use of it. My husband had already made out the plan for visiting and sight-seeing. The most important item in the list was to witness the 'Dak Exchange' between the two countries, at the international border, an exciting event to watch.

Exercise 'Operation Alert' had begun in the divisional sector, which further restricted the movement of families in the divisional sector. We were lucky; a special permission was granted to my husband from his higher headquarters, for visiting Nathula Pass, with a specific instruction not to sign in the visitor's book kept there at the Pass, for obvious reasons. I don't remember the day, could be Thursday; but definitely it was the day of *'Dak Exchange'*.

I am leading a Quwwalli at our unit Raising Day
Celebrations . I can'e believe myself .

Celebrating Holi with our unit officers families

At LoC with China

Nathula Pass 14,200 feet height?

It was a clear day. Blue sky with a few very patches of shining clouds against bright sun light, a pleasant day to visit Nathula Pass, we thought. The weather was cold, and it would be very cold and windy out there at the Pass, I knew. We were prepared, and had put on our warm clothing; in addition, we also took some from our unit and started in the morning after breakfast.

It was a long drive, over fifty kilometres from our present location at Five Mile. On our way up, he showed us their main regimental location at Thirteen Mile from the jeep.

Changoo Lake

A few kilometres further on the same axis, was **a beautiful lake called Changoo Lake, the biggest one in Sikkim,** I suppose. The road was going along the side of the lake; we got down from our jeep and spent a few minutes at the view point there.

The lake was quite big and was very calm; the road was continuing along the side of the lake for nearly half the shape of the lake. And the other half of the lake was touching very high cliffs. The lake had greater depth over a few hundred feet at places.

From the view point, we also got the view of the

Changoo Lake in Sikkim

Sikkimese Dolls.

Further on our way, we stopped at his company location at 'Twenty six Mile' stone. There again, we spent a few minutes just showing them around the place. There was a local primary school close to our company location, a small school building with a few class rooms. It had few divisions. Often, I saw kids from the near hutments going to the school, in their typical Sikkimese dress. With their chubby cheeks, small eyes and with their dress, they looked like Sikkimese dolls. The headmaster was very friendly; we, my husband and me visited the school and my husband and me and children distributed sweets to them and all felt very happy to be with them.

Our next stop was our destination, Nathula Pass. From our company location, we called up the unit headquarters responsible for defending the 'Pass' and informed them about our proposed visit to Nathula Pass. They gave us the green signal and also reminded me not to make any entries in the visitor's book kept at the Pass; because it was during the 'Operation Alert' that we were visiting and no families were permitted beyond 'Five Mile', during this period. And therefore, they did not want any documentary evidence.

It was a gesture, that they allowed us to visit the historically famous 'Nathula Pass'. We drove past the brigade headquarters, drove along high mountain road climbing up, following the contour till we came across a sign board showing the direction to Nathula Pass by an arrow. We followed that road; it was further climbing up and was leading to Nathula Pass.

As we climbed and went along the road, we got a glimpse of the Pass. Within a few minutes, we reached the base of Nathula Pass. Our vehicle was under direct observation from the Chinese observation post across the international border.

At the base, we were received by one of their sentries who escorted us to the top to their observation post. We climbed up a small hill through a covered walk way; it was something like climbing through a covered stair case. When we reached on top, Post Commander at Nathula welcomed us and guided to their observation post. Finally, we had reached the historically famous Nathula Pass between India and China, at a height about 14,200 ft. above MSL. Standing there, we felt as if we were standing on top of the world.

At Nathula Pass at 14,200 feet height

A view of the Chinese land across the Indo - China border post at Nathula

Our visit to Nathula Pass , the L o C with China at 14,000 feet height . One of our Greatest achievement

The observation post, there was a sand model of that general area, marking locations of both Indian and Chinese pickets.

Further, there were viewpoints, where arrows were fixed indicating directions to distant land marks, so that one could look in that direction and identify those locations. The most exciting thing was the view of Chinese observation post and their bunkers with the Chinese soldiers in their outfit, with their weapon, observing at our area from across the Line of Control.

It was at a 'stone's throw distance'/ at a talking distance. Their soldiers at their observation post had seen us coming up from the base and therefore, looked to be more anxious to get more details, so that they could reflect in their observation chart or situation report, as was done by our men at our observation posts. As they could watch our vehicles coming up to Nathula Pass, we could also see the movements at their side.

Our children and me felt very proud of their Dad, my husband for bringing us to such a place where very rarely one could reach. We thanked him. Standing at such a height, on the line of control between India and China, it was something quite unbelievable.

Dak Exchange at the International Border with China

My husband had briefed me about the 'Dak

Exchange' at Nathula Pass. This was an arrangement between the two countries, India and China, to exchange the 'Dak' (mail), meant for the local people across the border villages through a Dak exchange programme. It happened in once a week at about 11.a.m.

We, anxiously waited for that moment. The weather was good, sky was very clear and the sun was bright too; but it was very windy and chill at the Pass. An excellent day for anything. Through the binoculars, we saw all the area around very clearly, including distant mountains and defence structures there. Troops at those pickets spent their time mostly in observation posts during the day and at various 'listening posts' during night, first light/last light stand to, weapon cleaning and other maintenance or administrative activities. The Chinese soldier was still observing at our observation post from their side. We were waiting for the arrival of the postman.

We were not disappointed. A small pickup van came and halted at road, on our side. The postman escorted by a couple of armed soldiers got down from the vehicle; and walked up to the fence, marking the limits of the 'No Man's Land' from our side. These two armed soldiers took defensive position near the fence. When we looked on the Chinese side, from our observation post, we got a good view of the whole area, we saw a similar thing happening. It was 11.00 a.m.

Postmen from both sides, with a bag in their hand,

The Indian Side

The Chinese Side

Kachanachanjunga Peak t 8,600 meters , the
3rd Highest Peaak in the world

presumably the mail bag, started walking up to the 'Dak Exchange Hut'. On reaching there, they opened the doors on their side with the keys they had with them; and after entering the hut we saw our postman closing the door behind him. After a couple of minute or so, both the postman came out, again with a bag in their hand, this time presumably with the exchanged mail, locked the door from their side and walked down to the fence. When he reached the fence, the soldiers escorted him to the waiting vehicle and went away.

Depending on the weather and ground conditions, the postman was given enough time; for example, walking up in thick snow in

winters, definitely took much more time than walking over a bare ground on a clear day. Though a routine activity, these few minutes were of very anxious moments for the local Post Commander; because, anything could happen at any time.

Before leaving the post, with their permission, he took some beautiful pictures there, some of them with the Chines soldiers and Chinese observation post in the background. It was a rare occasion, destined to a few lucky and privileged class like us - very precious moments in our life.
I realised that it was a wise decision we took, after our marriage, to resign my teaching profession, to be with my husband throughout, wherever he was, with our children, able to enjoy the finest moments of life, to the full extent possible'.

On our way back, there was a vantage point along the

road from where we saw the shining, snow covered Kanchanjunga peak, the third highest peak in the world, nearly 8,600 metres high, of the great Himalayan ranges; an added achievement of our visit.

 The visit to Nathula Pass was a feather added to our cap. And those areas being restricted for civilian movement it is just next to impossible for a ordinary civilian to visit such places. But my husband being in the army even though it was a restricted period for visitors, he was given a special permission to visit Nathula Pass. Thus we were always considered as a privileged class. Visit to Nathula Pass was yet another feather on our cap.

Sikkim to Wellington in Nilgiris

Our Life journey continued. Form Sikkim we moved to Wellington some time during October 1984. We were there for almost three years. He was very lucky to get posted there only about five hours drive to his house. We had a very comfortable life there. It is a hill station. The weather was cool. We had bought our first car. We were all quite excited. Now, we could our homes in Kerala and we could also take our guests around, show them beautiful places around. Oh! We really had a jolly good time there.

Our children learning Computers

Our final house shifting to Thrissur

A Bold Decision

My husband is a unique personality. He has very good initiative and drive to do things. He is very positive and energetic. He is also very creative and innovative and he has many hobbies. He always found him very active all the time. He used to share his dreams about our family and about himself.

Once he mentioned to me that he was not satisfied with his army profession and he wanted to take premature retirement from the Army ad do something better outside. I knew my husband very well more than anyone else. I was also quite confident that whatever decision he took it will be always be the right decision, we would not have to regret in our life at all. In fact, I have been supporting him in all his activities. Here also I fully supported him.

After studying all the formalities, my husband submitted his papers for premature retirement for the Army after a period of twenty years. As I had mentioned, he was very punctual, systematic, well planned. Well it was like a miracle happened he got his release order within a matter of two months and he was released from the Army after 20 long years on 19 (AN) August, 1987

Thus, I lived nearly 17 long years with my husband while he was serving in the Corps of Engineers of the Indian Army., wherever he was posted and in whatever conditions he lived throughout his service we were always together.

Final Farewell Party organised by CWE(P) Wellington .

Presenting farewell momento to my husband

It ws a farewell for me too

Family gathering for the offlicers and families of his unit at our house

Our final house shifting from Wellington to Thrissur. Do you know, during our 17 years of family life together we had to shift our house 18 times, whenever my husband was posted from one unit to another unit. Oh, I just can't imagine the effort rquired to pack all the household stuff and after reaching the new location, we had to unpack and set them at our new location.

I found it very difficult. But my husband taught me how to pack each item individually and later pack them together in a big box. He also guided me how to make list of items packed in each box and mark all the boxes in serial order and to keep the details with me. This system really proved better as we could refer to the list of boxes and the items inside each box and decide which box we want to open first. This system helped us a lot for our house shifting during his transfers.

New Life Begins

After taking premature retirement from the army, we wanted to settle down at his home town, Thrissur. So, from Wellington, we finally said god bye to his Army life and came to Thrissur on 19 August 1987. N

The experience and exposure the army life had given to all of us had benefitted us a lot. Now each one of us including our two children had definite plan of action to begin our new life and move forward.

Our children, (one daughter and one son) are qualified, working professionals, married and settled in life. And husband and myself live in our own house, Glan Villa in our home town Thrissur. We were all happy at his decision and we looked forward his future plans.

I do not want to prolong this further. In short, after coming to our home city Thrissur, within a matter of a few months time he conceived, planned and executed and production started set up a Pharmaceutical Manufacturing Company by name, McGlan Pharmaceuticals (Pvt). Ltd. With a capital investment of Rs. 75 lakhs. And production commenced in a matter of eight months. Everything was e was the founder Chairman and Managing Director of this Company. Our daughter and me were also Directors.

After about 7 years he handed over our company to another management group. Later he worked abroad as a Senior Engineer with an International Construction Company in their very prestigious project, The Kingdom centre Tower Complex in Riyadh during 1998-99. He has also set up a Non-Profit Charitable Oganisation called Save A Life Foundation (SAL Foundation) in 2000. He is the Executive Director of SAL. SAL is being managed by our family.

My Inspiring Source

Here I would like to say that what I was at the time of our marriage and what I am today, all the 'change' I made which brought Success in my life are because of his inspiration. *My husband is the 'Inspiring Source' of my life.*

Jack of all Trades: Can you imagine a person doing all the trade works at home, as part of maintenance of our house?

Excellent Dog Trainer: I wish to mention about my husband is that he is an excellent

McGlan Pharmaceuticals - Dream Project, This Project designed, project completed in just eight months

Kingdom Centre Tower Complex , th intentional project my husband worksd in Riyadh

Dog Trainer. You will be quite surprise to see how trained all our pet dogs from their puppy stage till they were matured.

Our Dream Kitchen: Another thing, when we moved from our first Glan villa to our, present Glan Villa, kitchen was not up to our needs. Can you imagine, my husband totally removed our old kitchen and built a beautiful spacious, modular kitchen with lot of storage space.

Cooking: We get lot of mangos from our one mango tree. Once he found out recipe for some mango products, like Mango Jam, Sweet mango chutney, mango Pulp, hot and Sweet mango pickle, Mango halwa etc. and we make them every year.

Our Dream House -GLAN Villa: Very spacious house. Our Dream House was designed sand constructed by my husband only in mater of eight months. .

Learning is a Continuous Process. He always used to tell us and others also, that, learning is a continuous process and if you really want you can continue learning till your death. He is such a person; you can call him a moving encyclopedia.

He is a Published Author. He has many other activities also. He is a Published Author. Can you believe, He has many books to his credit

Our Dream House GLAN Villa

Our present house GLAN Villa

under different categories.

His Hobbies: In addition to all these, he has many major hobbies, like Photography, Numismatics, Philately, Painting, Singing, Driving, Gardening, Reading, Driving and so on. He also has three websites and two video channels on YouTube. Now a days he is quite busy in writing books.

He is very Creative: I do not know , how to express. He so creative that one can never imagine, as to how could he think of such an idea and make things. very recently he made a 'Coin art, using some coins for his coin collection.

He believes in Quality Time: At times he works for long hours. He is very good at time managing, I am quite surprised. He also believes in quality time. He finds time to do everything, to be with every one including our pet dogs.

Feeding Pigeons: You must be quite surprised to know, for the last 13 years, he has been feeding pigeons visit our terrace every day morning between 8 and 8.30 .a]And daily he goes up to the terrace and feed them. Oh, it is a sight. Our neighbourhood is excited about his activities.

Age is a Number Game for him: He is 74 plus now; but he doesn't realise that he is getting older, At least I feel, I have become old. I am tired and when I look back at my past life, I feel

Save A Life (SAL) Foundation Integrated Community development Project activities.

Kingdom Centre tower Complex Project my husband was wrking at Riyadh

Our Dream Kitchen

Our Pet Dogs Family

Listening to me

Our Mango products - mango jam, mango pulp,

more tired. We both have some ailments. his right eye has BRVO a retina problem and in spite of all these, on an average he spends about 4 to 6 hours with his laptop. And if he is writing a book then, on an average he works for 6 to 8 hours daily and at times even up to 10 to 12 hours.

In spite of that he is still very active. I am afraid how long will I be able to continue to support him.

About My Family

Before I conclude, I would like to mention a few things about my husband and our children.

My Husband: He always had some dreams to pursue and we have seen his happiness after realising his each dreams for example, about his Dream Profession, marriage, about becoming an engineer in life, to be able to live with his family, about his Dream Project, McGlan Pharmaceuticals (Pvt). Ltd., buying a conveyance for our family and his / our dream house. Having lived with him husband for over 49 years, I must say that my husband is a man of dreams, a person with 'Endless Dreams' not only he dreams but he works hard and realises his dreams. In way, I must say that it is this Endless Dreams, that have made him what he is today.

I do not have any words to express my feelings/ love, for him. He is so loving, caring and very protective about us.

Our Children: I must say that I am we are about our children. We wanted our children to grow, learn and do well in their life, like their day, my husband. Born and brought up in an army set up, travelling all over India, living and interacting with children with different culture and heritage had given them enough opportunities to learn a lot from their life. And the credit should be given to their Dad and Mom, and also continuously supporting them in their efforts to realise their Dreams. to do well in their life. I am quite happy, both our children, have done well, so far in their life. They are also married and settled down in their life.

Our Pet Dogs: I also like to mention about our Pet Dog family. You all know by now that our love for pet dogs began way back in 1971 when we took our puppy, Patty with us to Srinagar, who was a true companion to me during our stay at Srinagar. So far, we have had 12 pet dogs in our family. and we always considered them as part of our family. We all love them so much. Wherever we move they also moved along with. You may be quite surprised to know that during the 48 years of our life with our pet dogs, together, we had we have travelled together about 43,500 kilometres. Now they ar no more; but; they will always remain in our hearts.

Comparing myself in 1970 and now

I still remember my good old days till we got married. After we got married, it was his inspiration, support and guidance, which have made me what I am today. You know, he has taught me many things. Using his iPhone, I can take very good pictures and videos. And whatever I have done for my family, like, taking care of our children, taking care of our house, cooking, knitting, embroidery, stitching, tatting , all because of his inspiration, everything I do in my life, And one thing I want to tell you, he loves me, inspires me, supports me and during weak moments he strengthened me.

I just want to say, I am the luckiest woman in this world to get married to a wonderful husband like him. I could not have asked for more. I am what I am today is only because of him , just because of him. He was and he is my strength. It his inspiring words and support made me feel there is nothing 'impossible'. It is 'I'm possible'. He is my inspiration. And he is my inspiring source which made me make many Changes into my life.

He always tells his audience, a few things they should remember in their life to become successful:

* Always Dream and work hard and realise your Drams,

* You must have a will to learn, Will to work and Work hard – a three 'W' principles of life.

* Attitude is everything. Attitude towards your work and life that makes your life 100%

* So, change your attitude and we can change your life.

I am glad and contented that whatever I was at the beginning of our friendship the inspiring factor in him mas made me what I am today.

Let me conclude:
As my husband always tells his audience, we are all born to live to live our life. Life is something we define. We define its boundaries and the size of the field and the game we want to play was entirely up to us. So, please chose a game you like and play it well. You will be successful in your life.

I hope you enjoyed reading the exciting and emotional events of life.

Remember, 'Change' is inevitable in' Life'. And 'Change' makes 'Life a Success'! Good luck.

Husband Speaks

I am really glad to say a few words about my wife. "whether you believe her or not, I know her better that anyone else, not just because she is my wife; but she deserves respect and admiration for her. It's only because that I have written this book.

A young lady with timely CHANGES made in her life, what she is today. A loving and caring wife, a mother, very good housewife. She knows cooking knitting, stitching, tatting, gardening, can take very good picture and videos using my iPhone.

Another important quality about my wife is, she h can manage home finance very well. In fact, I hardly handled cash at home. She used to handle cash also keep a record of house expense and monitor the details. In addition to these, she is a Director of our Save A Life

(SAL) foundation, earlier she was also a Director of our McGlan Pharmaceuticals Pvt. Ltd. - Well travelled in India and also abroad and visited, Belgium, France, Holland, and Netherlands. She has played a major role in shaping and helping our children. Our eldest daughter is married and settled in Belgium and our son is also married an settled down in Bangalore.

I always believed that whatever strengths and weakness one may have, it is your life partner who can help to realise your dreams. And do you know "The secret of My Success?" I always wished for a Life Partner who,

> * Knows my likes and dislikes,
> * Knows my Strengths and Weaknesses,
> Understands my feelings and emotions,
>
> * Knows my Dreams and Aspirations,
> * Understands Family Values,   -
> * Respects others with dignity and
> * Gives me an Unconditional Support in

my life.

She has everything that I was looking for. And I used to tell my audience very openly about my wife: "She is 'Everything' in my life."

Our 70th Birthday was celebrated in 2015. Hope
to celebrate Wedding Golden Jubilee on 27th
April 2020

Thanks!